The Retreat of Reason

The Retreat of Reason

Political Correctness and the Corruption of Public Debate in Modern Britain

Anthony Browne

Commentary by
David Conway

Civitas: Institute for the Study of Civil Society
London
Registered Charity No. 1085494

First Published January 2006
Reprinted with minor corrections

Second Edition April 2006

© The Institute for the Study of Civil Society 2006
77 Great Peter Street
London SW1P 2EZ
Civitas is a registered charity (no. 1085494)
and a company limited by guarantee, registered in
England and Wales (no. 04023541)

Email: books@civitas.org.uk

ISBN-10 1-903386-50-0
ISBN-13 978-1-903386-50-7

Independence: The Institute for the Study of Civil Society
(Civitas) is a registered educational charity (No. 1085494) and a
company limited by guarantee (No. 04023541). Civitas is fin-
anced from a variety of private sources to avoid over-reliance
on any single or small group of donors.

All publications are independently refereed. All the Institute's
publications seek to further its objective of promoting the
advancement of learning. The views expressed are those of the
authors, not of the Institute.

Typeset by
Civitas

Printed in Great Britain by
Hartington Litho Ltd
Lancing, Sussex BN15 8UF

Contents

Shake off all the fears and servile prejudices under which weak minds are servilely crouched. Fix reason firmly in her seat, and call to her tribunal every fact, every opinion.

Thomas Jefferson, 1787

The cardinal sin, when we are looking for truth of fact or wisdom of policy, is refusal to discuss.

Sidney Hook, 'The Ethics of Controversy', 1980

Authors

Anthony Browne was born and raised in Cambridge, where he gained a mathematics degree. He has been economics correspondent for the BBC and the *Observer*, environment correspondent at the *Observer* and health editor at the *Observer*. He was environment editor at *The Times* and is now the paper's Europe correspondent.

His other books include *The Euro: should Britain join?* and *Do We Need Mass Immigration?* for Civitas, which was awarded Think Tank Publication of the Year in 2003 by *Prospect* magazine. He has also written papers on health policy for the Adam Smith Institute and on consumer policy for the Social Market Foundation.

He is a British immigrant living in Belgium with his Canadian wife and twin babies.

David Conway is a Senior Research Fellow at Civitas and Emeritus Professor of Philosophy at Middlesex University. His publications include: *Classical Liberalism: The Unvanquished Ideal* and *In Defence of the Realm: The Place of Nations in Classical Liberalism*

Personal Preface

There is not a truth existing that I fear or would wish unknown to the whole world.

Thomas Jefferson

It was a trivial event—the non-appearance of a pre-recorded interview on the BBC Radio 4's Today programme—that sparked the train of thought that led to this pamphlet. It wasn't just that the interview with me was dropped—an act of mercy on the listeners—but the contrast with the interview with a government minister that appeared in its place.

The episode was an example of the increasingly frequent avoidance of public debate in Britain—the 'politics of denial'—which is more than just a betrayal of the British public. The absence of debate also led the government to announcing an inappropriate policy that would do nothing to tackle the problems it was aimed at.

There was a conspiracy not so much of silence but of denial that stretched across the media and government from the lowest civil servants and reporters to the highest ministers and interviewers. There was endemic dishonesty towards the public, but because everyone was in denial to each other, few realised it because their virtual reality had become the widely acknowledged truth. This received wisdom was in fact easy to disprove—it just required looking at some government tables—but everyone had an emotional investment in not disproving it.

The collective denial so enveloped the media-political elite that they had little idea how detached their world-view was from reality. When I started putting the truth out in the public domain, I was met with an almost universally intolerant and intellectually dishonest response by people who preferred political correctness over factual correctness.

Even many of those who realised the intellectual honesty of what I had been reporting were unable to accept it emotionally, because for most people when intellect and emotion conflict, emotion wins.

The interview on the Today programme was on a highly sensitive subject—the exponential rise of HIV in Britain since Labour was elected in 1997. Figures from the government's Public Health Laboratory Service were being published showing a 25 per cent rise in just one year, with almost all the increase being among heterosexuals. The government and media had been warning for years about the dangers of the new complacency among heterosexuals, ever since the number of heterosexual cases had swept past the number of homosexual ones, a well reported and much commented-on phenomenon. The government minister was responding on the Today programme to the latest increase with a new sexual health campaign telling people to practice safe sex. If teenagers would just wear condoms, it would put a stop to the rise.

But the trouble is that the increase in HIV had virtually nothing to do with British people practicing unsafe sex—it was almost all the result of HIV positive people (mainly Africans) coming to the UK, and being diagnosed with HIV once here.

I first wrote about the issue in a front page story in *The Times*, announcing that African immigration had overtaken gay sex as the main source of new HIV cases in Britain, according to government figures. The government's epidemiologists with whom I had worked on the story had been worried about the reaction. They needn't have bothered. The reaction was incredulity. Clearly, in most people's minds, the story couldn't be true—everyone knew the increase in HIV was because of complacent and promiscuous Britons.

The Department of Health's director of communication, when I spoke to her about it, clearly thought I was bonkers —she was launching this safe sex campaign because everyone knew the rise in HIV was the result of unsafe sex.

The only people who phoned me up to thank me about it were HIV doctors, who lived in the real world, not the politically correct virtual one. Their patients were now predominantly (and sometimes exclusively) African immigrants, and yet no one was talking about it. Some doctors told me that when they had tried to bring it up in public with their local health authorities, they had just been shouted at.

One of the government's own medical advisers phoned me up secretly from within the Department of Health thanking me for highlighting the issue, and urging me to carry on: Britain was facing a massive explosion in HIV and ministers and civil servants simply refused to discuss the cause of it. 'Ministers just won't listen because they think it is racist' he said, 'but the public deserve at least honesty.'

Even when the truth became intellectually commonly accepted, media outlets such as the *Guardian* and BBC carried on reporting dishonest accounts, presumably because they had such deeply held emotional beliefs in the issue that they couldn't bring themselves to write honestly about it. A cover story I wrote for the *Spectator* was directly attacked by a news story in my old paper the *Observer*, whose desire to disprove what I had written trumped their inability to do so.

In fact, although their tone was often somewhat sensational, the most intellectually honest media outlets tended to be Britain's much maligned tabloid media. It isn't the only time that Britain's tabloids, so hated by the left, have actually been the torch-bearers for truth by daring to write deeply uncomfortable things that others refuse to.

Two years after my front page story in *The Times*, the denial about the whole issue of HIV finally crumbled. The Public Health Laboratory Service now openly reports that

African immigration is the main cause of new HIV in Britain, and even left-wing media are enabled to report it.

One person told me that, even if it is true that the HIV epidemic is driven by African immigration, it shouldn't be written about because it will just fuel racism. But the result of that conspiracy of silence is that the government follows a policy that does absolutely nothing to combat the growth of HIV in the UK. Tackling the epidemic will fuel racism far less than allowing African immigration to spark an HIV explosion, a development allowed by government policy which is a political gift to the racist British National Party.

The one definite benefit is that the lives of HIV positive immigrants are saved. But if the cost of NHS treatment were spent in Africa, not the UK, it would save between 10 and 100 times more lives.

There is also the human cost: the HIV epidemic that is being imported from Africa is now being transmitted within the UK. In fact, the majority of people who contract HIV from heterosexual sex in Britain are actually catching it from having sex with HIV positive African immigrants. In total, nearly 1,000 people have caught HIV from infected immigrants since Labour came to power, ironically finally giving a rationale to the government's safe sex campaign. That's 1,000 lives blighted, ultimately, by political correctness. Those who defend political correctness must accept that it can come at a heavy price.

But this book is not about the epidemiology of HIV. It is about the intellectual and emotional processes behind that debate, and how they apply across the public discourse and policy spectrum in twenty-first century, politically-correct Britain.

Summary

For centuries Britain has been a beacon of liberty of thought, belief and speech in the world, but now its intellectual and political life is in chains.

Members of the public, academics, journalists and politicians are afraid of thinking certain thoughts. People are vilified if they publicly diverge from accepted beliefs, sacked or even investigated by police for crimes against received wisdom. Whole areas of debate have been closed down by the crushing dominance of the moralistic ideology of political correctness.

Political correctness started as a study of cultural Marxism in Germany in the 1920s, and was adopted by the 1960s counter culture, eager to promote tolerance and alternatives to the conservative values of the time.

Political correctness quickly infiltrated US academia and spread its tentacles across the West. By the early twenty-first century, political correctness had completed its long march through the institutions in Britain, and had ensnared almost all of them, from schools to hospitals, from local government to national government, and from major corporations to the police, army and the church. In 1997, Britain became governed for the first time by a government largely controlled by politically-correct ideology.

Its influence has spread across the entire policy range, not just women's pay and race relations, but education, health, law and order and the environment. It is upheld by a powerful array of lobby groups, from Liberty to Amnesty International, from Friends of the Earth to Refugee Action, and an array of domestic and international laws, charters and treaties.

Starting as a reaction to the dominant ideology, it has become the dominant ideology. It defines the terms and parameters of any national debate. Anything that is not PC is automatically controversial. Across much of the public sphere, it has replaced reason with emotion, subordinating objective truth to subjective virtue.

In the early days, political correctness brought benefits as it helped spread decency and consideration to the more vulnerable members of society, from the handicapped to women to ethnic minorities.

But, as political correctness spread and deepened its influence, it became more dogmatic and intolerant of dissent, until it became a betrayal of the very liberalism that first fuelled it. It has lead to new political censorship laws being introduced to curb freedom of speech, and membership of legal democratic parties being curtailed. Rather than opening minds, it is closing them down.

The aim of political correctness is to redistribute power from the powerful to the powerless. It automatically and unquestioningly supports those it deems victims, irrespective of whether they merit it, and opposes the powerful, irrespective of whether they are malign or benign. For the politically correct, the West, the US and multinational corporations can do no good, and the developing world can do no wrong.

Political correctness is often ridiculed, but it is more than just a joke. With its earlier benefits already won, it has now become a hindrance to social progress, and a threat to society. By closing down debates, it restricts the ability of society to tackle the problems that face it.

PC promoted multiculturalism in the Netherlands while silencing debate about its drawbacks, until the results exploded in religious violence leaving much of the country living in fear. In Britain, it allowed the creation of alienated Muslim ghettoes which produce young men who commit mass murder against their fellow citizens. By promoting the rights of criminals over their victims, it hinders law enforcement and leads to escalating crime. By challenging the authority of teachers, it fuels poor discipline in schools, and by promoting equality over excellence, it degrades the standard of education and inflates exam grades until they become almost meaningless.

By silencing debate and curbing objective analysis, political correctness can harm those it intends to help. The victims are taught to blame others for their vulnerability, discouraging them from taking responsibility for improving their lives if their problems are self-inflicted.

Black communities are encouraged to blame racist teachers for the failure of their boys at school, rather than re-examine their own culture and attitudes to education that may be the prime reasons. The poor sick have ended up having worse healthcare in Britain than they would in mainland Europe because PC for long closed down debate on fundamental NHS reform. Women's employment opportunities can be harmed by giving them ever more rights that are not given to men. The unemployed are encouraged to languish on benefits blaming others for their fate. Poor Africans are condemned to live in poverty so long as they and their governments are encouraged to blame the West for all their problems, rather than confronting the real causes of poor governance, corruption and poor education.

Political correctness once had a purpose, but it now causes much more harm than good. For the last few decades, reason has been in retreat—but the time has come for reason to advance once again.

1

What is Political Correctness?

He does not seem to know what an argument is. He never uses arguments himself. He never troubles himself to answer the arguments of an opponent... It has never occurred to him... that when an objection is raised, it ought to be met with something more convincing than 'scoundrel' or 'blockhead'.

Lord Macaulay, 'Essay on Southey's Colloquies'

The phrase 'political correctness' conjures up images of left-wing councils banning black bin-bags, nativity scenes being banned by the Red Cross and handicapped people being called 'otherwise-abled'. Some of these cases, such as renaming firemen as firefighters, merely reflect a changing reality. Others are just the most overt symptoms of political correctness, and easily ridiculed: he's not dead, he's metabolically challenged.

But political correctness is more than a joke or updating of historic language usage. It is a system of beliefs and pattern of thoughts that permeates many aspects of modern life, holding a vice-like grip over public debate, deciding what can be debated and what the terms of debate are, and which government policies are acceptable and which aren't. It has grown in influence over the last few decades to the extent that it has now become one of the most dominant features of public discourse, not just in Britain, but across the Western—and particularly the Anglophone—world.

The irony of political correctness is that it is itself almost politically incorrect. Few people like to think of themselves as politically correct, and fewer still would dare publicly admit to it. It is a term generally only used by its detractors.

PC is also surprisingly unexamined as a phenomenon, the subject of few academic treatises and few books, at least outside the US. Criticism of it has rarely graduated from ridicule to analysis.

Part of the problem is that there is no standard definition of political correctness. Peter Coleman, a former Australian government minister from the Liberal Party, wrote:

> Political Correctness is a heresy of liberalism. It emerges where liberalism and leftism intersect. What began as a liberal assault on injustice has come to denote, not for the first time, a new form of injustice.[1]

He said that it was liberalism that has been taken over by dogmatism, that it is 'intolerant', 'self-righteous' and 'quasi-religious'.

The Politically Correct are more intolerant of dissent than traditional liberals or even conservatives. Liberals of earlier generations accepted unorthodoxy as normal. Indeed the right to differ was a datum of classical liberalism. The Politically Correct do not give that right a high priority. It distresses their programmed minds. Those who do not conform should be ignored, silenced or vilified. There is a kind of soft totalitarianism about Political Correctness.[2]

The US conservative commentator Paul Weyrich, the President of the Free Congress Foundation, is also exercised by the intolerance of political correctness, although his main concern is its antipathy to Western values:

> The United States is very close to becoming a state totally dominated by an alien ideology, an ideology bitterly hostile to Western culture. Even now, for the first time in their lives, people have to be afraid of what they say. This has never been true in the history of our country. Yet today, if you say the 'wrong thing', you suddenly have legal problems, political problems, you might even lose your job or be expelled from college. Certain topics are forbidden. You can't approach the truth about a lot of different subjects. If you do, you are immediately branded as 'racist', 'sexist', 'homophobic', 'insensitive', or 'judgmental.'[3]

The US commentator William Lind, director of the Centre for Cultural Conservatism, is among those who have described PC as 'cultural Marxism', declaring that it is 'Marxism translated from economic into cultural terms'.[4] He wrote:

> The cultural Marxism of Political Correctness, like economic Marxism, has a single factor explanation of history. Economic Marxism says that all of history is determined by ownership of means of production. Cultural Marxism, or Political Correctness, says that all history is determined by power, by which groups defined in terms of race, sex, etc., have power over which other groups. Nothing else matters.[5]

The *New York Times'* culture correspondent, Richard Bernstein, who came out against multiculturalism in his book *The Dictatorship of Virtue*, was also concerned about how PC tried to overturn the dominant culture and power structures. In a landmark 1990 article which sparked debate about PC in the US, he wrote:

> Central to pc-ness, which has its roots in 1960s radicalism, is the view that Western society has for centuries been dominated by what is often called 'the white male power structure' or 'Patriarchal hegemony.' A related belief is that everybody but white heterosexual males has suffered some form of repression and been denied a cultural voice.[6]

These are all largely descriptions of characteristics of political correctness (discussed at length in chapter 2) and its method of working, rather than a definition of it. Dictionaries tend to give it descriptive, and sometimes circular, definitions. In his political dictionary, William Safire defines political correctness as:

> Conforming to liberal or far-left thought on sexual, racial, cultural or environmental issues.[7]

Others see political correctness as little more than a form of civic gentility. The *Wall Street Journal* gave the definition:

> Political correctness, for all its awfulness, is an effort to save souls through language.[8]

For those who believe in liberal democracy and the market-place of ideas, there should be nothing wrong in attacking western culture and traditional hierarchies, insulting men, promoting homosexuality, or trying to redistribute power. Those that don't agree can openly argue back.

The problem with political correctness comes when liberal democracy and its foundation, freedom of speech, come under attack; when the market-place of ideas, rather than offering a wide range of views, offers any view so long as it's PC.

This is the most troubling aspect of political correctness, and what separates it from most other systems of belief. The most useful definition of political correctness is one which defines it by its intolerance of dissent, dictating that which is 'correct' and that which is 'incorrect': I suggest the following:

DEFINITION

Political correctness is an ideology that classifies certain groups of people as victims in need of protection from criticism, and which makes believers feel that no dissent should be tolerated.

There are many beliefs—usually based on reason, evidence and free debate—that tolerate dissent, ignore it, and sometimes even actively encourage it. Liberal democracy is utterly dominant in the West, and yet co-exists easily with those who do not believe in it, such as communists, anarchists and religious fundamentalists— until such time, as with radical Islamists, as they threaten its very survival. Science, and in particular empiricism, is dominant, but rarely bothers trying to silence those who hold unscientific beliefs such as the paranormal, alter-native medicine and astrology. It just laughs at them.

Christianity is also the dominant religion in the West, which in the last century has done little to try to stifle

4

dissent, but rather tolerates and even welcomes growing non-Christian minorities.

The rise of political correctness represents an assault on both reason and liberal democracy. It is an assault on reason, because the measuring stick of the acceptability of a belief is no longer its objective, empirically established truth, but how well it fits in with the received wisdom of political correctness. It is an assault on liberal democracy, because the pervasiveness of political correctness is closing down freedom of speech and open debate (see chapter 6).

For the modern mind, confronted with a new set of policy options on a difficult issue, the first reaction is not to try and divine the right answer, but the 'politically-correct' one. Many people will think first of what the true answer is, and in an effort to avoid controversy or offence, measure it up against the dictates of political correctness. Those whose intellectual faculties have been all but closed down by political correctness have learnt to automatically short-cut to the PC response.

Potentially politically incorrect arguments, whether valid or specious, are made more palatable by transposing them into politically correct arguments with the same conclusions to make them more acceptable. The Royal College of Nursing officially opposes the mass recruiting of nurses from the developing world to work in the NHS because of the impact it has on Third World health services, rather than the impact it has on its own members in keeping downwards pressure on pay and conditions, and numbers trained to be nurses.

In both public and private, people prefer to make politically correct arguments even if they know them to be wrong, than to make politically incorrect arguments that they believe to be right. Making a wrong argument which is safe is widely preferred to making a right argument which is unsafe.

The precaution is, in the calculus of personal damage limitation, entirely rational: people who transgress politically correct beliefs are seen not just as wrong, to be debated with, but evil, to be condemned, silenced and spurned. Moral cowardice has led to intellectual dishonesty permeating and corrupting our public debates.

Across much of Britain's public discourse, a reliance on reason has been replaced with a reliance on the emotional appeal of an argument. Parallel to the once-trusted world of empiricism and deductive reasoning, an often overwhelmingly powerful emotional landscape has been created, rewarding people with feelings of virtue for some beliefs, or punishing with feelings of guilt for others. It is a belief system that echoes religion in providing ready, emotionally satisfying answers for a world too complex to understand fully, and providing a gratifying sense of righteousness absent in our otherwise secular society.

The result is that public figures sanctified as being politically correct (the high priests of PC, such as Michael Moore) are listened to with reverence on any potentially controversial issue, safe in the knowledge that even if what they say suffers the insignificant drawback of being wrong, it will at least enjoy the far for important benefit of being PC.

The politically incorrect arguments aren't engaged with; they are just stated in a way that everyone will understand means it is unacceptable because it is not PC. 'He believes women win fewer Nobel prizes because of genetic differences between men and women' is deemed a conclusive rebuff to the evidence that there are differences to men's and women's brains. When Larry Summers, the president of Harvard University, mildly suggested innate differences in ability between men and women may account for the differences in achievements at the summits of academia, he was met with walk-outs, denunciations and demands for resignation by people who offered no actual proof that he was wrong.

Because the politically correct believe they are not just on the side of right, but of virtue, it follows that those they are opposed to are not just wrong, but malign. In the PC mind, the pursuit of virtue entitles them to curtail the malign views of those they disagree with. Rather than say I would like to hear your side, the politically correct insist: 'you can't say that'.

Believing that their opponents are not just wrong but bad, the politically correct feel free to resort to personal attacks on them. If there is no explicit bad motive, then the PC can accuse their opponents of a sinister ulterior motive—the unanswerable accusations of 'isms'. It is this self-righteous sense of virtue that makes the PC believe they are justified in suppressing freedom of speech. Political correctness is the dictatorship of virtue.

The end result is that the politically correct build impregnable castles around their beliefs, which means, like royalty, never having to justify and never having to apologise. As the Norwegian playwright Henrik Ibsen, a champion of free thinking, wrote:

> Castles in the air—they are so easy to take refuge in. So easy to build, too.[9]

In the topsy-turvy politically correct world, truth comes in two forms: the politically correct, and the factually correct. The politically correct truth is publicly proclaimed correct by politicians, celebrities and the BBC even if it is wrong, while the factually correct truth is publicly condemned as wrong even when it is right. Factually correct truths suffer the disadvantage that they don't have to be shown to be wrong, merely stated that they are politically incorrect.

To the politically correct, truth is no defence; to the politically incorrect, truth is the ultimate defence. To the politically correct, the 'truth' is no longer 'something that exists in objective reality' but 'something that supports my pre-held beliefs'. This selective definition of truth makes PC arguments almost impossible to refute.

Issue	Politically Correct Truth	Factually Correct Truth
Women's pay less than men's	Sex discrimination	Different work/life choices, Childcare breaks
Explosion in HIV	Teenagers having unsafe sex	African immigration
Rise in anti-Semitic attacks	White skinheads	Muslim youths
Africa getting poorer	West not giving enough aid	Bad governance

In consequence, the politically correct often believe you can justify their version of truth with a lie. When the *Mirror* published photos purporting to show UK soldiers torturing Iraqis, the paper's supporters still justified them after they were proved to be fake on the grounds that they illustrated a greater truth (which they apparently did, but no one would be excused for illustrating a politically in-correct truth with a lie). Michael Moore fabricates facts with merry abandon in his films, and yet his supporters are unapologetic on the grounds they represent the (politically correct) truth.

In contrast, when Robert Kilroy-Silk wrote that Arabs were 'suicide bombers, limb amputators, women repress-ors', he wasn't sacked by the BBC because it wasn't true as a description of the most disturbing features of some contemporary Arab societies, but because it broke the laws of PC. The BBC declared that it 'did not share' Kilroy's views, an implicit acknowledgement that even though as an institution it is not meant to have its own views, it by default adopts politically correct institutional beliefs. Despite the fact that government figures show that Afro-

Caribbeans commit disproportionate numbers of violent street crimes compared to other ethnic groups, people are denounced if they say so in public.

Counter arguments to politically correct beliefs are dismissed without consideration, or simply suppressed. When the *Observer* and the BBC denounced the tyranny of the government for locking up foreign suspected terrorists without trial in Belmarsh Prison, they rarely mentioned that the suspects had defied government orders to leave the country, that despite being in prison they were free to leave Britain to any country that would take them, that many had already done so, and that the government didn't deport them forcibly to their home country because to do so would be a breach of their human rights under the Human Rights Act. To admit any of this would undermine the politically correct's attempt at creating a sense of outrage by portraying it as a simple case of a powerful Western government abusing powerless non-Western citizens. Belmarsh was not Britain's Guantanamo: the inmates of Guantanamo cannot leave and are outside the democratic rule of law, a rather important distinction.

The Redistribution of Power

But what is the point of political correctness? Why are some things politically correct, and others not?

At its most fundamental, political correctness seeks to redistribute power from the powerful to the powerless. At its most crude, it opposes power for the sake of opposing power, making no moral distinction between whether the power is malign or benign, or whether the powerful exercise their power in a way that can be rationally and reasonably justified.

The only reason that it is more politically correct for religious fundamentalists to deliberately kill as many innocent civilians as possible (Hamas suicide bombers) than for a liberal democracy (Israel) to selectively kill the terrorist leader responsible for the wave of suicide bombers (Hamas founder Ahmed Yassin) while trying to avoid the loss of innocent life, is because the Israeli government is strong, and the Palestinians weak.

America, as the world's most powerful country, can never do any good, even though it is the world's most powerful liberal democracy, the largest donor of overseas aid, and it defeated both Nazism and Communism.

The West, as the world's most powerful cultural and economic group, can safely be blamed for all the world's ills, even though it is largely responsible for the worldwide spread of prosperity, democracy and scientific advance.

Multinational corporations are condemned as the oppressors of the world's poor, rather than seen as engines of global economic growth with vast job-creating investments in the world's poorest countries, pushing up wages and transferring knowledge.

Conversely, political correctness automatically supports the weak and vulnerable, classifying them as nearly untouchable victims, irrespective of whether they merit such support or not. When the successful, affluent, powerful Dutch film maker Theo van Gogh was ritually murdered in the streets of Amsterdam for insulting Islam, the politically correct, including the *Guardian* and Index on Censorship, automatically sided with the comparatively powerless Islamic Dutch-Moroccan killer.

The way that PC distorts news values was shown in the comparative coverage of the murder of 52 innocent people by Islamic extremists in Britain's worst ever terrorist attack, and the killing of an innocent Brazilian immigrant by British police a fortnight later. After a few days, the coverage of the terrorist attack was obliterated by saturation coverage of the accidental police killing, much to the anger of relatives of the London bombings. The reason was simply that the terrorist attacks, although a far more important story, didn't fit the politically correct agenda, whereas the killing of a vulnerable immigrant by a powerful police force did.

The extent to which PC subordinates moral considerations to considerations of power is shown by the PC response to the extraordinary spectacle of Iraqis celebrating the first free democratic elections in their lives under the auspices of the US, and being threatened with being blown to bits for the simple act of voting by a coalition of Islamic fundamentalists and fascist Baath party supporters. Even the most cursory ethical consideration would show it is right to support ordinary Iraqis trying to choose their own government, over those who want to kill them for practicing that democracy. But the fact that the elections are supported by the powerful US and opposed by the comparatively powerless fundamentalists causes problems for the PC. Opposing power for the sake of opposing power, many of the politically correct left—including the *Guardian*, the *Independent*, most of the BBC and the former Labour MP George Galloway—have chosen to champion those who are deliberately trying to murder innocent civilians.

Automatically opposing the powerful and supporting the powerless means that, when presented with a new issue, the politically correct must decide not what is right or wrong, malign or benign, true or untrue, but who is the more powerful and who the less powerful. The PC analytical process enjoys the beauty of simplicity:

1. identify the victim.

2. support them and their interests, irrespective of any other factors.

Thus in a dispute between China and the US, the politically correct will tend to support China; but in a dispute between China, and, say, Tibet, they will automatically (and rightly in this case) support Tibet.

Sometimes perceptions of relative power between groups change, and then the PC change their allegiances. Britain's politically correct used to support the white working class, seen as the victims of oppression by the middle classes; but then they discovered that the white working classes were higher up the power hierarchy than more vulnerable ethnic minorities, and so started openly targeting their ire at the white working classes (as chronicled in Michael Collins's book *The Likes of Us*). Even though the white working classes themselves hardly changed, the change in perceptions of power in society meant that attacking the white working classes suddenly went from being politically incorrect to politically correct.

The same transposition of power has happened between Jews and Muslims. Since the Holocaust, Jews have often been portrayed as the ultimate victims, and anti-Semitism as the ultimate bigotry. But in the early 2000s, partly as a result of the intifada—where the Jews are seen as oppressors rather than the oppressed—and partly as a result of rising concerns about Islam after September 11th, Muslims became the ultimate victim group, and Islamophobia the greatest bigotry.

This dual role of Jews as both oppressors and oppressed causes complications for PC calculus, but the transposition of power relations means that PC has now firmly transferred its allegiance from Jews to Muslims.

This transfer of allegiances was confirmed by the European Monitoring Centre on Racism and Xenophobia, which commissioned a report on anti-Semitism in Europe, and then suppressed it when the authors concluded that the main cause of rising anti-Semitism in Europe is Muslim youths, not skinheads and neo-fascists. The EMCR told the authors, who were Jewish, that the report would undermine their work helping Muslims, who are the most discriminated-against religious group in Europe, and told them to rewrite it to portray the main perpetrators as white racists. When the authors protested that was contrary to the evidence, the EMCR rewrote the report itself, and published it with a summary and conclusion that was at total odds with the evidence actually contained within it. At the press conference, the EMCR repeatedly stated that white skinheads were to blame, despite the evidence inside the report and the views of the researchers. The *Independent* newspaper followed the politically correct line with an article headlined: *White men blamed as attacks on Jews rise.*[10]

In stark contrast, the *Telegraph* ran a less politically correct but more factually correct article, with the headline: *EU 'covered up' attacks on Jews by young Muslims.*[11]

Since victims are supported not because they are right but because they are vulnerable, critically questioning them is seen as attacking them, and those who do so are vilified as oppressors. In the world of PC, victims can say anything or ask for anything, not because they are right or deserve it, but because they are safe from public scrutiny or objection.

The most overt racism, sexism and homophobia in Britain is now among the weakest groups, in ethnic minority communities, because their views are rarely challenged, as challenging them equates to oppressing them. PC's inherent contradictions make it largely incapable of resolving such objectively simple ethical problems such as the murderous homophobia of Jamaican rap singers or the cruelties of forced marriages. The Labour government tolerates the numerically far greater animal cruelty of halal slaughter and bans the far less significant cruelty of fox hunting simply because the perpetrators of halal slaughter have victim status while fox hunters have oppressor status.

Few things are more powerful in a public debate than publicly acknowledged victim status, and the rewards for public victimhood are so great that there is a large incentive for people to try to portray themselves as victims. Thus the victim class grows bigger as more try to crowd into it, and others copy their tactics. At the beginning of twenty-first century in Britain, the obese, Christians, smokers and fox-hunters are campaigning to achieve publicly acknowledged victimhood, with the hunters trying unsuccessfully to turn PC on its head by declaring they are the real victims of 'prejudice'. Advances in medical diagnosis have meant that boys who would previously have been considered naughty and in need of discipline are now considered victims of Attention Deficit-Hyperactivity Disorder in need of support and treatment.

In the battle between emotion and reason, emotion wins most of the time for most people: the heart trumps the head because it is more difficult to live with bad feelings than bad logic. Few are the souls tortured by bad reasoning; many are those tortured by guilt. However overwhelming the evidence, people believe what they want to believe, and find it very difficult to believe what they don't want to.

The easiest way to overcome the dissonance between what you want to believe and the evidence is not to change what you believe, but to shut out the evidence and silence those who try to highlight it. Until the recent election of a right-wing government in Denmark, it was illegal to publish crime figures broken down by ethnicity of offender.

People tend to believe that which makes them feel virtuous, not that which makes them feel bad. Most people have a profound need to believe they are on the side of virtue, and can do that by espousing beliefs publicly acknowledged as virtuous. Nothing makes multi-millionaire Hollywood actors who live in Beverley Hills feel better about themselves than campaigning against world poverty by demanding more aid from the West (rather than holding African leaders responsible for the plight of their people by demanding better governance).

But what is virtuous about this? One of the ironies of political correctness is that, since it subjugates objective truth to subjective virtue, it often causes more harm than good (see chapter 6). Good intentions pave the road to hell. The world is not short of good intentions, but it is too often short of good reasoning.

2

The Hallmarks of Political Correctness

Lack of Faith in Human Nature

The politically correct have limited faith in human nature, seeing it as essentially flawed, and hold a belief in its perfectibility with sufficient psychological re-engineering. The African-American academic Thomas Sowell defined it as the difference between the 'constrained' view of human nature by those who accept its essential flaws, and the 'unconstrained' view of those who believe human nature can be perfected.[1] Those with a constrained vision tend to be more pragmatic and right-wing, those with the unconstrained vision more Utopian and left-wing.

The politically correct believe that people can be made caring, selfless and tolerant, and to see themselves as citizens of the world rather than their country. The politically incorrect may believe that culture and society is improvable—for example in the way that women and homosexuals are treated—but believe there are limits to how much you can change human nature, and that some basic flaws should be accepted and could even be useful.

Political correctness is in this sense very much like Marxism, which believed that personal greed and selfishness could be eradicated from the human character, and that people could be educated to work as hard for the common good as for their personal good. Likewise, multiculturalism transfers the quest for human perfection from the economic sphere to the social and cultural one, requiring people to give up feelings of tribalism and belonging, and requiring them to prefer 'the other' to the familiar.

Marxism, it should be noted, failed because it failed to perfect human nature; belief in multiculturalism is now doing likewise.

Promotion of Re-Education

The Utopian quest to perfect human nature drives the promotion of re-education, from the classroom to the workplace. It occurs in PC children's books, which are sometimes rewritten timeless classics that are no longer deemed acceptable. (*Snow White and the Seven Dwarfs*, all of whom were also white, is unthinkable nowadays.)

It occurs in the school curricula, which now include such treasures as Black History Month and Gay, Lesbian and Transgender History Month, where history is rewritten on the flimsiest (and even non-existent) evidence that national icons such as Florence Nightingale and William Shakespeare were homosexual.

In workplaces across the country, from companies to army bases, from hospitals to TV stations, people are being subjected to 'diversity training' to re-educate them and make them more politically correct. Across the spectrum of TV programmes, multiculturalism is vigorously promoted.

Like the belief in the perfectibility of human nature, the passion for propaganda and re-education has powerful similarities to the practices of communist societies. While Soviet Socialist Realism promoted the virtue of the proletariat, the BBC promotes the virtue of the multicultural society.

Lack of Faith in Democracy

Distrusting human nature, and wanting to perfect it, puts limits on the politically correct person's faith in democracy. They often justify limits on democracy by saying that if democracy were too direct, then Britain would still

17

have hanging and homosexuality would still be illegal (although both assertions are questionable; direct democracy would promote debate and understanding). The PC dismiss their opponents as 'right-wing populists', as though there was something inherently wrong in being popular in a democracy (there is a considerable difference between being a populist, and being a hatemonger). Political correctness drives many of the curbs on democracy, as discussed in chapter 6.

The PC's lack of trust in democracy is justified: most people privately object to political correctness. Given how out of touch the PC elite are with the people, democracy is the worst enemy of their most treasured beliefs. When viewers of the ITV programme *Vote for Me* finally chose someone to stand as a politician, it was Rodney Hylton-Potts, who promised to halt all immigration to Britain, and who was denounced as a 'comedy fascist'.

The novelist Frederick Forsyth wrote that political correctness:

> is insultingly patronising and contemptuous of what it describes as 'ordinary people'. It is a creed for a self-arrogated elite. Anything that is popular is described as 'populist', a derogatory adjective referring to the lowest of tastes. Deriving from this, it is antidemocratic; while affecting to approve democracy, it much prefers its own self-awarded elitism. Politically, it prefers government of the few, by the few and above all for the few.[2]

Support for Censorship

Their conviction that those they oppose are not just wrong but malign, and their desire to perfect human nature, not only leads the politically correct to a distrust of democracy, but also to support censorship. This desire to curtail the speech of opponents they deem offensive ranges from 'no platform' policies to overt legal censorship, as detailed in chapter 6.

Liberal Guilt

One of the most powerful psychological foundations of political correctness is liberal guilt. Many in the West from middle-class backgrounds suffer a usually unspoken guilt about their unearned privilege, which in turn can lead to an under-current of self-loathing in their views. Men often feel guilty about being men, and whites often feel guilty about being white, even though these are innate characteristics they can do little about. Men may support women-only university colleges, for example, because it appeases their male guilt, rather than a real belief that they are necessary at a time when more women than men already go to university and on average get better degrees.

When the former BBC director general Greg Dyke described the BBC as 'hideously white', what explains the word 'hideous' apart from liberal guilt? Asians are now over-represented in law schools and medical colleges, but no one, let alone another Asian, would dream of calling law schools and medical colleges 'hideously Asian'. No Afro-Caribbean would call Brixton 'hideously black'.

When Western adults were doing their bit to promote unsustainable world population growth, the West was full of guilt-ridden treatises, leading to a range of pressure groups and charities campaigning to reduce birth rates. It was easy to campaign on: the end of the world was our fault. Now that the population of the West has stopped growing, concern about overpopulation has become very unfashionable because, as Tony Benn put it, it means wanting fewer brown babies. The combination of Western guilt and fear of racism has all but killed off public concern about overpopulation in the last few decades. In the US, when population growth was caused by white people having too many babies, the country's largest environment group, the Sierra Club, campaigned to control population. But now that US population growth is mainly caused by immigration, it has dropped all policies on population, and indeed its funding is dependent on never trying to tackle the immigration issue.

Liberal guilt never feels more satisfied than when it is self-flagellating. The euphoria over the Live 8 concert—and the wall to wall coverage given by the media—was only possible because it followed the politically-correct line that African poverty is not the fault of African despots and culture, but our own fault for not being generous enough with aid and not writing off debt. This guilt is not only patronising—saying the Africans aren't able to develop by their own efforts—but also misplaced: no country has risen out of poverty by means of aid and cancelled debts. From China to South Korea, India to Malaysia, they have developed out of their own efforts, with aid being at best marginal.

The 'it's all our fault' line of reasoning—and the soft racism it peddles—was beautifully illustrated in a 'more-politically-correct-than-thou' article on Jamaican homophobia, entitled 'Their homophobia is our fault' by Decca Aitkenhead. She said that Jamaican homophobia was the result of 400 years of Jamaican men being sodomised by their white slave owners, and rather than Western campaigners urging Jamaicans to stop murdering gays, she wrote:

> A better emotion would be culpability. Every ingredient of Jamaica's homophobia implicates Britain, whose role has maintained the conditions conducive to homophobia, from slavery through to the debt that makes education unaffordable. For us to vilify Jamaicans for an attitude of which we were the architects is shameful. To do so in the name of liberal values is meaningless.[3]

Getting Western white liberals to self-flagellate offers an easy way out of the PC conundrum of whether it is acceptable to tell poor black Jamaicans to stop murdering homosexuals. But Rob Berkeley, of the UK's Black Gay Men's Advisory Group, replied:

> Today's Jamaicans are responsible for today's anti-gay abuses. They are, like everyone else, capable of rational thought and

ethical choices. Those who are homophobic are not compelled by history or poverty to be anti-gay. To suggest that the people of Jamaica cannot change laws and values inherited from the British colonial era is to infantalise them.[4]

Psychologising Arguments

Instead of addressing the explicit content of an argument, the politically correct attack what they see as the hidden psychology behind the argument: their opponents are not just wrong but bad. Accusing someone of hidden and malign motives avoids the often intellectually and emotionally difficult task of engaging with their actual arguments, and allows the politically correct to remain protected in their castle on the moral high ground.

If a white opposes affirmative action for blacks, they are assumed to be driven by racism even though many blacks also oppose affirmative action (one of the difficult truths for the politically correct). If a man argues that differences in pay between men and women are an inevitable consequence of different lifestyle choices and different legal entitlements to retirement and parental leave, he is automatically assumed to be driven by sexism.

Those who said it was counterproductive to give money to street beggars were simply reviled as mean spirited and selfish, until many homeless charities came out in agreement. Someone who argues that some forms of limited whaling can be justified on conservation and animal welfare grounds is considered anti-nature. Someone who claims that prison works is assumed to be cold-hearted, unable to comprehend the difficult lives of criminals.

Ad Hominem Attacks

The inevitable consequence of psychologising arguments is *ad hominen* attacks, attacking the arguer rather than the argument. Those who question the politically correct shibboleths are deemed a viable target for any personal abuse in either public or private. Those who critique politically correct nostrums are often denounced as extreme.

The need to be protected against *ad hominem* attacks means that only women can attack feminism, only Muslims can attack Islamic fundamentalism, and only those with a proved commitment to the treating the sick-poor can criticise the NHS.

Guilt by Association: the Personal Form

Just as in Senator Joe McCarthy's excessive hunts for communists, or the Soviet Union's attempts to root out dissidents, the politically correct have a tendency to assume guilt by association. If someone is deemed guilty of a thought crime, then anyone linked to them is often also considered guilty. This guilt by association argument has a very powerful effect in isolating those who break politically correct taboos because even closet sympathisers don't want to be publicly associated with them.

Guilt by Association: the Intellectual Form

The politically correct have a tendency to oppose arguments not on their own merits, but on the grounds that they have been associated with other arguments or people which are taboo. 'That's what the National Front said' is often used to dismiss the argument that immigration can have an impact on the labour market opportunity and wages of some native workers, even though many of the world's top labour and immigration economists have produced much econometric evidence that supports the claim. The truth or otherwise of arguments doesn't depend on who supports them, nor on what arguments they have been linked with in the past. It makes as much sense as telling vegetarian conservationists to change their ways on the grounds that Hitler was a vegetarian who loved nature.

Preference for the Personal rather than Abstract

Being based primarily on emotion rather than reason, the politically correct prefer the personal in an argument rather than the abstract. This is not just making arguments personal by using *ad hominem* attacks, but telling personal stories, particularly hard luck cases. These personal stories, which work well for TV, may shed light on a general issue, but often they don't. Concentrating on the horrors faced by a starving African child will induce a sense of guilt in Western readers, but it gives no clue to whether the child is starving because of corrupt governments and lack of rule of law, or because the West is not giving enough aid.

Powerful Victimhood

Political correctness grants a special status to those whom it deems the victims of the established power structures in society, or those who claim they are. A victim of domestic violence is deemed to be an automatic expert on it, even though someone who walks out of an abusive relationship before violence occurs is probably more worth listening to. One consequence of the power of victimhood in the US is the new phenomenon of race attack hoaxes, whereby people fabricate racist attacks against themselves (see chapter 4).

Promoting Group Identities

Classifying someone as a victim or oppressor before considering the rights or wrongs of an argument is much easier if you divide humanity up into groups of victims, identified and united by their victimhood: blacks, Muslims, gays, women, disabled. Classifying humanity into group identities almost automates the PC thought process: Woman = victim = right; man = oppressor = wrong.

It is only one step further from attributing group identities to giving people rights on the basis of those

23

group identities (so long, of course, as they are victim groups). If you are black or Asian, you may have a right to affirmative action to help you enter higher education or desirable careers. But such group identities can be inherently unjust—middle-class Asians can be born with far more advantages in life than working-class whites. Judging people by the group they belong to rather than who they are also just replicates the prejudice that the PC fight: it is the basis of discrimination and racism.

The politically correct have become so obsessed with defining people by their group identity that they require everyone to classify what group they belong to, and for the institutions they attend to classify them. As part of the inexorable logic of PC, students, patients and employees are now pigeonholed into categories such as black, white, or Asian. Police forces have even been required to ask recruits whether they are homosexual or not—a gross intrusion into their private life—so they know what group box to tick.

Judging people by the group they belong to makes them more likely to be seen as little more than products of that group, and less likely to be seen as individuals, responsible for their own destiny. It is, ultimately, not just patronising, but dehumanising and counterproductive. It is the vulnerable who refuse to be pigeonholed who escape their vulnerability.

Double Standards

If all powerful people were malign and all vulnerable people benign, there would be no conflict between reason and political correctness, between supporting what is right and supporting those who are weak. But they are not, and there is. That conflict between reason and political correctness often leads to extraordinary double standards.

There are countless groups, associations and publications based on ethnicity which would be unacceptable if they were working for whites. For example, the Society of Asian Lawyers actively promotes the career opportunities of lawyers solely on the basis of their Asian ethnicity, while Tower Hamlets recently opened an 'Asian only' housing development.

Men are (still) openly legally discriminated against in terms of retirement rights in a way that would be utterly unacceptable if it applied to women, despite the fact that men live shorter lives and thus would be expected to retire earlier.

Although European enslavement of Africans is endlessly commented on, the Islamic world's enslavement of Africans (and to a lesser extent Europeans) is rarely discussed, even though it has occurred on a similar scale (less intensively but over a longer period) and is still ongoing. From a slave's point of view, who enslaves them is less important than the fact that they are enslaved; the West's refusal to confront contemporary Islamic slavery is a reflection of the inability of PC thinking to engage a non-PC reality.

As Peter Tatchell, a man of such uncompromising principles that he has infuriated many on the relativist left, said about Ken Livingstone's open embrace of the homophobic, misogynist, terrorism-supporting Sheikh Yusuf al-Qaradawi:

> Livingstone argues that he welcomed the cleric because he is a major religious leader. Would he greet a Christian fundamentalist who advocated, as al-Qaradawi does, the creation of a theocratic state where democracy and individual liberty would be erased, where gay sex would be punishable by death, where wife-beating would be permitted and where free speech, trade unions and the right to protest would be crushed?[5]

Left-wing activists have campaigned hard and passionately against the Israel's occupation of the West Bank, while being almost totally silent on the Syrian occupation of Lebanon, and pretty mute on the Chinese occupation of Tibet. The double standards, and targeting just of Israel, is not because Israel is worse than the others, but because PC calculus has trouble condemning Arab and Chinese dictatorships and finds it easy to condemn democracies.

The double standards of PC have ensured that communist dictators, such as Stalin, are treated far more leniently than fascist ones such as Hitler. This is not explicable by the number of deaths they caused: in the twentieth century, communism (in the Soviet Union, China and South East Asia) was responsible for far more deaths than fascism.

Extremism

The elimination of critical opposition means that PC is often taken to extremes. Sometimes this is an insistence on 'zero tolerance', but sometimes goes beyond. Isolated from any tempering voices of reason, the politically correct in local authorities and academia can take their views to extremes that to outsiders are simply ludicrous. The canteen of the School of Oriental and Asian Studies upbraided one German student for asking for white coffee because it could be construed as racist: she was told to ask for coffee with milk.

Taking Offence

The intolerant, sanctimonious moral superiority that sustains the beliefs of the politically correct means that they are easily offended by the views of others. There are few as intolerant as those who preach tolerance. In contrast, if your beliefs are upheld by reason and empiricism, then opposing views don't offend you, they intrigue you.

Lack of Sense of Humour

With its *ad hominem* attacks, psychologising, zero tolerance, extremism and preference for censorship, political correctness is well protected from most forms of intellectual assault. But none of them work against humorous satire, the soft underbelly of political correctness. The politically correct can resist jokes at their expense by stamping their foot and saying 'it's not funny', but satire can be far more potent.

In the United States, conservative students found that the only way to attack affirmative action—whereby students are admitted to university on the basis of skin colour, as under apartheid—was to satirise it. Copying affirmative action programmes that automatically give lower entrance thresholds for members of ethnic minorities or women, conservative students set up stalls selling cookies for $1 to men, 50 cents to women, and 25 cents to African Americans.

Fox News reported:

> Through Affirmative Action Bake Sales, conservative groups on campuses across America are satirically and peacefully spotlighting the injustice of Affirmative Action programs that penalize or benefit students based solely on gender and race.

> The sales are intended to spark discussion, not profits. They are in the same genre as guerrilla theatre—an effective counterculture tactic usually associated with the Left—through which societal assumptions are challenged by acting out scenarios. To the amazed query, 'Are you allowed to do this?' one cookie rebel responded, 'Admissions officers do it every day'. By shifting the context from university policy to baked goods, the assumptions of affirmative action policies are not only challenged as sexist and racist but also revealed as nonsense.

> The cookie rebels are doing the one thing political correctness cannot bear: revealing its absurdity and laughing in its face. They are not merely speaking truth to power; they are chuckling at it.

> To regain the moral indignation they prize so highly, the politically correct must demonize the sale of baked goods. Thus, at Indiana University one student filed an official complaint saying that the cookie sale would 'create a climate of hostility against students of color and women and can easily turn violent'. (The fact that those students were the ones given a price break didn't seem to occur to the irony-starved critic who equated a buyer's discount with a threat of violence.)

> The College Republicans at the University of Washington sponsored an affirmative action bake sale on 7 October. CR

President Jason Chambers reported: 'Approximately 150 students were gathered around our booth discussing the issue [AA] by about 12:30 when our booth was attacked by leftist students who disagreed with our stance on affirmative action.' The Leftists threw cookies to the ground, tore down the display and physically attacked one vendor.

The University of Washington is not alone.

- The University of California-Irvine shut down its bake sale as discriminatory.
- Northwestern University ordered students to cease selling cookies or face the police.
- Southern Methodist University closed the bake sale after 45 minutes because it created an 'unsafe' environment.
- William and Mary officials—claiming to be 'shocked and appalled'—also cut off the cookies.

Clearly, universities don't like the affirmative action bake sales. One reason: The sales, like that at Indiana University, often feature petitions 'to ban the collection of racial data, particularly in the admissions and hiring processes'.

But most of all, the politically correct do not like being publicly mocked and revealed as ridiculous.

3

The Origins of Political Correctness

A lie told often enough becomes the truth.

Vladimir Lenin

Intolerance is as ancient as human belief. Christianity, particularly in eras of religious persecution such as Elizabethan England, has shown many of the characteristics of modern political correctness, and often went far further by enforcing its intolerance with violence (as does Islam in parts of the world today). Darwin became the victim of a Victorian form of political correctness, when he was lampooned and shunned for saying that our ancestors swung from branches.

Intolerance has often applied outside religious issues. Those who challenged existing power structures, such as demanding women's right to vote, in Victorian England, would have been treated in much the same way as those who now break PC taboos.

But the Enlightenment, and advocates of liberty and freedom of thought such as Mill, Locke and Voltaire, started the opening up of the human mind and gradually put an end to 'politically correct' religious beliefs, allowing free and open dissent. During the last century, the human mind has become more open than any previous period, but it is now closing down again.

Modern political correctness is usually thought to have originated at the 'Frankfurt School' in inter-war Germany. William Lind[1] wrote that it started when the Institute for Social Research at Frankfurt University, founded in 1923, started transferring Marxist techniques from economic to cultural and social issues, and adding elements of Freud. One of its founders, George Lukacs, said its purpose was

29

answering the question: 'who shall save us from Western civilisation?' With the rise of Nazi Germany, many of the leading lights of the 'Frankfurt School' fled to the US, and their way of thinking rapidly gained influence in the US academia, which has long been the stronghold, and main propagator, of PC.

Political correctness is thought to have gained strength out of disillusion among western communists with the Soviet Union. No longer able to mount a credible challenge to Western capitalism with economic arguments, they transferred their attacks on the West to its culture.

The real growth in influence of political correctness came with the 1960s counter-culture, when the widespread liberal desire to challenge the conservative rules governing society proved a fertile breeding ground for PC ideology. Coleman described PC as the intersection between the left and the liberal, but added that the hard-line ideology of PC triumphed over the *laissez-faire*, rebellious liberalism. The result is that PC turned 'the liberalism of the 1960s into a dogmatic and conformist, even bullying, ideology'.[2]

It was the turning of tolerance into intolerance that provoked Frederick Forsyth to describe political correctness as 'the new fascism':

> I loathe and despise political correctness; basically because it is a lie. It is a lie because it purports to be one thing while being the opposite. It began as a philosophy begging for greater tolerance and no right-minded person could object to that.
>
> Tolerance—of other people, of minorities, of different appearances, habits and views—is the angel dust that marks the difference between a barbaric and a civilised society.
>
> But PC has changed. From its original plea for tolerance of variables in what Malraux called 'the human condition', it soon began to adopt a conviction of rigid self-righteousness. Long since, it has developed into a new and intolerant bigotry, the very thing it was supposed to oppose.
>
> PC now tolerates no dissent from its grinding uniformity, from its party-line-toeing orthodoxy. It smacks of Orwell's *1984*, or former East Germany; it has become the new fascism.[3]

The literary scholar John Ellis notes in his book *Literature Lost: Social Agendas and the Corruption of Humanities* that Western intellectuals have been finding fault in their own societies and perfection in others since the Roman historian Tacitus eulogised the Germanic people in the first century AD. Although known as barbarians, Tacitus said they were unusually democratic, unsexist, maritally faithful and avoided vices such as pride and gluttony. The eighteenth-century Franco-Swiss philosopher Jean-Jacques Rousseau popularised the vilification of Western civilisation with his romanticising of the 'noble savage'. Ellis claims that the politically correct, by uncritically praising the non-West, are proving just how Western they really are:

> political correctness itself is a thoroughly Western phenomenon. From earliest times, Western society has been prone to recurring fits of this self-doubt. Those who are seized by this mood may imagine that they are taking an anti-Western stance, but that is all part of the same pattern of self-delusion.[4]

Post-modern philosophy, which has emphasised cultural relativism and played down objective reality, has also fuelled political correctness. As Howard Schwartz, Professor of Organisational Behaviour at Oakland University, wrote:

> When the idea of an objective external world is lost, the idea of achievement, of earning love on the basis of good work, no longer has meaning. Individuals who have had status in the past, and who legitimated that status by claims of achievement, come to be seen instead as having acquired their status illegitimately. The idea of gaining status through achievement comes to be seen as a smoke-screen for theft. Those who have had status are thus redefined as having stolen love from those of low status. They are seen as oppressors who deserve to be hated and attacked, and to have their power destroyed.[5]

4

The Triumph of Political Correctness

Despite its counter-culture and possibly Marxist origins, political correctness has now become the dominant ideology of the West. But just how far does its influence extend? And how did it progress through the institutions and minds of the West?

Some junior members of the British aristocracy may hold 'colonial and natives' fancy dress parties in the year 2005—and even that was almost certainly just an anti-PC tease—but in the rest of the country, PC has completed a pretty clean sweep imbedding itself through all the institutions, from school to TV broadcasts, from company HQs to the army. It is difficult to think of any part of life— certainly public life—that has not succumbed to the dictates of PC. The first black Archbishop of York has declared that the Church of England is institutionally racist.

Political correctness came to national prominence in the 1980s, but it was only a decade later that people started becoming concerned about its advance. In the widely debated Letter to Conservatives in 1999, Paul Weyrich, the conservative commentator, stated:

> it is impossible to ignore the fact that the United States is becoming an ideological state. The ideology of Political Correctness, which openly calls for the destruction of our traditional culture, has so gripped the body politic, has so gripped our institutions, that it is even affecting the Church. It has completely taken over the academic community. It is now pervasive in the entertainment industry, and it threatens to control literally every aspect of our lives.[1]

Complaints about it taking over the academic community in the US are well founded. Studies of multiculturalism, racism and sexism have in many institutions overtaken the traditional Judaeo-Christian canon. US textbooks in public schools and colleges have to have 'sensitivity vetting' to check they are politically correct. A whole series of books such as Allan Bloom's *The Closing of the American Mind* has charted the transformation. The former White House policy analyst and American Enterprise Institute fellow Dinesh D'Souza wrote:

> The transformation of American campuses is so sweeping that it is no exaggeration to call it an academic revolution.[2]

In Australia, the former government minister Peter Coleman described the pervasiveness of PC:

> Its first and pre-eminent characteristic is that it calls for the politicisation—one might say the transformation—of life. It wants political direction of all departments from, say, children's fiction to judicial judgments. No profession is exempt. All must meet a political test—of correct thinking and progress. Lawyers, accountants, doctors, scientists, novelists, journalists and businessmen must all pass it.[3]

In the US, Lind wrote in 2004:

> The ideology that has taken over America goes most commonly by the name of political correctness. Some people see it as a joke. It is not. It is deadly serious. It seeks to alter virtually all the rules, formal and informal, that govern relations among people and institutions. It wants to change behaviour, thought, even the words we use. To a significant extent it already has.[4]

So much has political correctness become the established ideology, that the traditional roles of Right and Left have been reversed. The Right has traditionally represented the established status quo against the revolutionary assault of the Left. But the PC Left has now become the establishment, so that, as the Cincinnati University academic Herbert Shapiro wrote:

> The Right presents itself as the defender of intellectual freedom against a Left that would close off the dialogue of ideas. The American university is now portrayed as though under the domination of the radicals.[5]

In 1997, Britain began, in effect, to be ruled by political correctness for the first time. The Labour government was the first UK government not to stand up to political correctness, but to try and enact its dictates when they are not too electorally unpopular or seriously mugged by reality, and even sometimes when they are. The previous Conservative government was almost deliberately politically incorrect, and during the previous Labour government political correctness had too little grip on the body politic to hold much sway.

In Britain, at the start of the twenty-first century, political correctness encompasses almost the entire range of policies from women's pay to race relations, health care to education, crime to child discipline, and almost every institution, society, company and authority.

Political correctness has gained power over public services, from schools and hospitals to local authorities and central government. Political correctness became institutionalised at the BBC, but also started exerting control over ITV and broadsheet newspapers. Politically correct alternative comedians quickly swept to power, becoming the new establishment, while PC triumphed in the literary field. PC triumphed not just in trade unions and charities, but in professional and trade associations, from medical Royal Colleges to business associations. Finally, even multinationals and the police started succumbing to PC.

The long march of PC through every nook and cranny of national life, leaving nothing untouched, was helped by the fact there is little competing ideology: although PC has been ridiculed, there has been virtually no counter-PC movement. A society enjoying unprecedented affluence and no external threats can afford to become intellectually decadent.

PC's methodology of controlling speech and isolating opponents has been extraordinarily effective in a society that has practiced free speech for so long—and had to fight for it so little—that it has become complacent about it.

Since its establishment as the national ideology, political correctness sets the ground rules for debate, and is the benchmark against which public opinion is measured. When two strangers meet and talk politics, the need for acceptance means that more often than not they will usually stick to the politically correct text, even if they don't agree with it. So heavy is the punishment for transgression that few mainstream politicians or public figures would dare to be un-PC unless there is huge electoral advantage. Those simply seeking popular approval, such as actors or pop stars, automatically adopt and espouse politically correct beliefs, reinforcing them in the public mind in the process.

Anything that breaches political correctness is automatically controversial, and so any institution that wants to court public acceptance and avoid controversy must be PC. Since most institutions in Britain want to be publicly accepted, most have now become thoroughly permeated by political correctness.

The broadcast media, and the BBC in particular, stick to the politically correct text on most issues because it safely protects them from criticism. The BBC can endlessly promote mass immigration against the wishes of its licence fee payers with impunity, but as soon as one Panorama programme pointed to some downsides of mass immigration, it was attacked by the government and left-wing press as being 'Powellite'. The film industry, both in the UK and US, almost uniformly sticks to the safe territory of promoting political correctness.

PC has silenced many awkward debates, as well as those that oppose them. As the row over Charles Murray's book *The Bell Curve* showed, the study of racial differences has become almost totally taboo. Groups such as the Southern Poverty Law Centre have proved very effective at silencing those they deem guilty of 'hate'.

Amnesty International has been turned by political correctness from a worthy fighter for political prisoners around the world into a knee-jerk anti-Western-government campaigning organisation that has all but lost sight of its founding principles. Index on Censorship is on the brink of turning from an organisation that campaigns for freedom of speech to one that campaigns against it.

Political correctness has also created a climate that has fuelled a vast growth in charities and pressure groups that support and promote the politically correct world view on almost all issues. From Greenpeace to Amnesty International, from Refugee Action to the National Council for One Parent Families, a huge non-governmental sector has grown up, all pushing in the PC direction. They are often taxpayer-funded, or charities subsidised by tax relief, and can campaign for funds from the public without opposition. They are given endless invaluable free publicity from the BBC and most newspapers as objective, independent groups—the BBC repeats everything that Liberty says with such unquestioning respect that they treat it often as a justification for a story in itself, with no counterbalancing points of view, even though Liberty is tied closely to the Labour party and cannot be described as politically neutral. As frequently complained about in the tabloid media, the National Lottery has been reduced to a fund to promote political correctness.

Non-government groups that may have a politically incorrect aspect to their work usually silence it. The Council for the Protection of Rural England campaigns about house building in the countryside, but it would never dare tackle one of the main, and most easily tackled, causes in the growth in housing demand, mass immigration.

In contrast, there are virtually no pressure groups that promote politically incorrect views, and most of those that do, such as Christian family groups, tend to have a low profile and are treated with suspicion by the media, especially the BBC. One example is Migrationwatch UK, founded by the former ambassador Sir Andrew Green, a lone group campaigning for less immigration (a view supported by 80 per cent of the public), against literally dozens of groups promoting mass immigration. In contrast to these other groups, Migrationwatch gets no taxpayers' money and is almost totally blackballed by the BBC, and to some extent by the broadsheet media. Political correctness also means that high profile figures are far less likely to support Migrationwatch in public than they are any politically correct organisation, because they will automatically become open to attack.

Political correctness also succeeds, like the British empire, through divide and rule. While those on the politically correct side of a debate can happily hang together, whatever their differences, the politically incorrect often end up appeasing political correctness by denouncing fellow travellers, in an act of 'triangulation' aimed at making them appear less extreme than the others. Political correctness is so powerful, and the guilt by association that it promotes so effective, that even the politically incorrect fear being seen together. This makes it far more difficult for politically incorrect individuals and groups to work together for common causes.

Changes in society have fuelled the growth of political correctness. The growing emphasis on emotion and feelings over reason and logic in recent decades, combined with the decline in the study of science, has given PC a more powerful grip on the mind of the nation. The triumph of a more superficial celebrity culture over an intellectual literary culture has reduced resistance to PC, as shallow celebrities are more likely to succumb to the fashionable pressure of being PC than an intellectual icon. The TV culture champions the personal experience over abstract reasoning, intrinsically giving backing to politically correct ways of thinking.

PC encourages policies that further increase its potency. It encourages Third World immigration to the West, importing challenges to traditional Western values, and dividing society into ethnic groups where identity and grievance politics can thrive. It encourages the growth of the public sector, increasing the domain where it has the most powerful grip.

Political correctness also binds its values into the fabric of a country by laws and international treaties that make it very difficult to challenge. Various human rights laws, charters, conventions and treaties, from the UN to Europe to the Human Rights Act, create an entire international and domestic legal framework that upholds PC values and beliefs, making it very difficult for future governments to challenge them. When Michael Howard, the Conservative leader, said in 2005 that if elected Prime Minister he would take Britain out of the UN convention on refugees, he was told by the European Commission that he had no legal right to, and Britain would immediately be taken to the European Court of Justice.

Ultimately, political correctness is the luxury of a powerful society. As the fear of Islamic terrorism has shown, PC's enemy is a society's sense of vulnerability. When people feel insecure, they more strongly resist what they see as the idiocies of PC because they believe the stakes are too high.

The combination of all these factors meant that PC, one of history's most wide-ranging ideological revolutions, enjoyed the most extraordinarily rapid advance. Ellis wrote:

> Dissenters can expect to be not only criticised, as dissenters always are, but denounced as both moral outcasts and unsophisticated simpletons. Yet this is done on the basis of a viewpoint that coalesced far too quickly for it to have been properly thought through, one that seemed to advance not by its intellectual force but instead by a kind of tidal action that suddenly surged everyone. It is time to retrace our steps, to do what should have been done initially; we must take a hard look at what this position really

amounts to and whether it is sound enough to deserve the commanding position it now has.[6]

5

The Benefits of Political Correctness

The worst enemy of truth and freedom in our society is the compact majority. Yes, the damned, compact, liberal majority.

Henrik Ibsen, 'An Enemy of the People'

Those that dare support political correctness usually suggest, somewhat meekly, that 'it does have a purpose'. As Angus Roxburgh wrote:

Political correctness, so derided by all the politicians of the far right, developed for a reason: it is the product of civilisation, and reflects a basic desire to tolerate, not persecute, those who have different faiths, beliefs, or skin colour.[1]

To the extent that it can modify thoughts and behaviour in individuals, political correctness helps stop the strong abusing the weak. It is a powerful weapon to promote basic decency of behaviour, when simple courtesy has failed. It stops white football crowds shouting racist abuse at black footballers, it stops employers refusing to employ homosexuals, and it stops the able-bodied jeering at the disabled. It encourages people to open their minds to those who are different rather than simply stereotyping them, such as East Enders seeing their Sikh neighbours as people rather than as turban-wearers.

Political correctness can ameliorate the institutional callousness of large organisations, too often blind to the needs of non-mainstream groups, from access to the disabled to the hiring of ethnic minorities.

One of the main purposes of civilisation is that it protects the weak and curbs abuses by the strong. Few could oppose the basic underlying aim of political correctness, to redistribute power from strong to the weak, just as to some extent the role of government is to redistribute wealth from the rich to the poor.

6

The Drawbacks of Political Correctness

Political Correctness is a really serious danger to political health.

Saul Bellow

Freedom to think as you will and to speak as you think are means indispensable to the discovery and spread of political truth...[We know] order cannot be secured merely through fear of punishment for its infraction; that it is hazardous to discourage thought, hope and imagination; that fear breeds repression; that repression breeds hate; that hate menaces stable government; that the path of safety lies in the opportunity to discuss freely supposed grievances and proposed remedies; and that the fitting remedy for evil counsels is good ones.

Justice Louis Brandeis,
concurring in Whitney v. California (1927)

As well as its benefits, political correctness has draw-backs, and the more that political correctness strengthens its grip on the minds of policy makers and opinion formers, the more drawbacks it has.

At the start of the twenty-first century, most of the benefits of political correctness have already been banked —the basic promotion of equality for women, homo-sexuals, disabled and ethnic minorities. With diminishing returns to the benefits, political correctness is now causing far more harm than good.

Although the redistribution of power from the strong to the weak can provide definite benefits, taken to extremes it can cause damaging unintended consequences. Aristotle believed that every virtue is associated with two vices, one by an insufficiency of the characteristic related to that

41

virtue, the other by excess. Redistributing wealth from rich to poor leads to a more equal, fairer and more harmonious society, but, as the failure of communism showed, excess of redistribution leads to economic stagnation, widespread poverty, poor quality of life and endemic demoralisation. Denunciations of xenophobia, jingoism and racism are necessary, but taken to excess lead to the destruction of any sense of national identity that produces social solidarity.

Political correctness promotes the creation of a 'victim mentality', discourages people from taking responsibility for their own lives, suppresses free speech, and distorts public debate, leading to bad policies being adopted.

It can be so extreme that it harms even those it is supposed to help. Women can have their employment chances in the workplace harmed by giving them ever more rights than men, making it rational for employers to discriminate against them; the vulnerable are encouraged to live rough on the streets by charity handouts which create a street culture, tempting them away from hostels where they can be helped more effectively; the unemployed are encouraged to languish on benefits rather than find a job by a welfare system so comfortable that it can make work financially unattractive; young black males have their education harmed by being encouraged to blame others for their failure rather than setting higher goals for themselves and taking responsibility for their lives; ethnic minority children can have their life and employment chances damaged by not being required to learn English and integrate more into mainstream society.

Creation of a 'Victim Class'

The redistribution of power from the strong to the weak can be so great as a result of political correctness that many people find it rational to campaign to make themselves appear vulnerable in the eyes of others.

Achievement of 'victim status' can lead to considerable rewards—apart from soothing sympathy, you can avoid being openly challenged by others, accusing those who challenge you of an 'ism' or 'phobia', and attract special treatment and benefits from policy makers.

Victim status is best achieved by tirelessly promoting the damage that 'society' does to you, while trying to silence those who would challenge you. Campaigners trying to achieve the full benefits of victim status on behalf of a group of people do so by exaggerating either the scale or the seriousness of the problem.

The scale of the problem can be increased either by simply inflating the numbers affected, or diluting the definition of victim to such an extent that far more people are drawn into it. Thus women's campaigners have claimed that one in four women is the victim of domestic violence by including verbal abuse, while disability campaigners claim one in eight people is disabled by broadening the definition of disabled to such an extent that it includes many people who would probably see themselves as perfectly able, thank you very much.

One of the most successful campaigns for victim status has been by Muslim groups in Britain, notably the Muslim Association of Britain, which increases its clout by inflating the number of Muslims in Britain by a million more than the official census, and by accusing anyone who tackles its extremist Islamist agenda of 'Islamophobia'. Although it has a thoroughly oppressive agenda (supporting terrorism against innocent civilians, promoting the rights of husbands to beat their wives and the execution of gays), the MAB passes itself off as oppressed so convincingly that it has fooled the PC establishment, notably the *Guardian*, *Independent* and BBC, into promoting it unquestioningly.

In Britain, but more notably in the US, smokers and obese people are campaigning to achieve victim status. The smokers have an uphill battle, but groups representing obese people are succeeding in blaming everyone but themselves for their weight, and thus winning some sympathy as victims of society, and of discrimination.

The desire to become a victim can be so strong that, in extreme cases, people even fabricate evidence of victimhood. In the US, and France, there have been many well documented cases of people making up stories of racial attacks in order to engender sympathy. In one US case, a black teacher smashed up her own car and accused white racists of doing it. After witnesses said they saw her smash up her own car, she confessed, but still won widespread support because the principle of victimhood remains (the truth not being the ultimate defence for the politically correct).

When the creation of victim status coincides with direct financial rewards, the results can be explosive. Even race campaigners complain that it allows 'knaves to use racism as a poison to destabilise and terrorise organisations',[1] sometimes making false accusations of racism to extort money. In parts of the Ukraine, where officially recognised victims of the Chernobyl disaster were given free health treatment, accommodation, holidays and generous monthly benefits, half the population claimed they were victims of radiation, even though medical studies suggested the numbers were in the low thousands.[2] In parts of Wales, a quarter of the working population have succeeded in registering themselves as officially disabled in order to claim larger benefits.

Political correctness can lead to 'competitive victimhood', which leads to tensions between groups that were otherwise living harmoniously as they compete for prime victim status. Howard Schwartz noted that the 'subordination of truth to goodness' led to a situation where:

> instead of competing for achievement, students come to engage in a competition for sympathy and even pity. By showing that they have been victimized, oppressed, abused, devalued in the past, the

students assert their claims to compensatory appreciation and resentfully depreciate the claims of others. From this standpoint, we can understand the development which balkanizes student bodies into hyphenated groups proclaiming their competing histories of oppression and grievance.

This emotionally charged conflict, when it takes place in our intendedly multicultural universities, undoubtedly is a source of constant surprise, perplexity, and sadness to the well-meaning individuals who have given rise to it. But by establishing narcissism as the norm for university life, PC advocates made it inevitable that the actual university would be the locus of bitterness, envy and ill-will. Resentment and hostility are not just temporary feelings which will be outgrown in the PC university; they are built into its very structure.[3]

Perverse Incentives: the Rewarding of Vice and the Punishing of Virtue

Almost by its very nature, political correctness undermines the age-old incentive structure that has driven progress in society, whereby virtues such as hard work, discipline and education are rewarded with success and wealth, and lack of such virtues is punished by failure and poverty. In contrast, political correctness rewards victim status, encouraging people to strive to be recognised as victims, and scorns (and sometime even encourages discrimination against) successful people who are deemed oppressors.

By encouraging people to strive for the bottom rather than the top, political correctness undermines one of the main driving forces for progress in society, the individual pursuit of self-improvement. Political correctness can be, quite literally, unprogressive.

Political correctness tells the weak and vulnerable that it is society that is wrong and needs changing, not themselves. Sometimes this is true, but just as often it is not.

If someone is poor because they are systematically oppressed by the rich, who distort laws to entrench their wealth and deny opportunities to the poor, then the sentiments of political correctness are entirely right: the poor should be supported against the rich, and laws should be challenged.

If, however, someone is poor because they are lazy, ill-disciplined, addicted to benefits and resentful of those who aren't poor, then encouraging them to blame other people rather than emulating them, and supporting their self-inflicted harm through generous benefits, will in fact just perpetuate their poverty. Political correctness can entrench poverty rather than offer a route out. Blaming others will prevent them changing how they behave, which is the only way they can stop being vulnerable. By preventing uncomfortable self-examination and justifying self-harming behaviour, political correctness harms those that it purports to support.

Someone who is poor for these self-inflicted reasons needs the precise opposite of political correctness: they need to be encouraged to copy others, rather than blame them, and they need their self-harming behaviour and attitudes to be challenged rather than comforted.

Probably the most extreme example is that of Australian aborigines, whose initiative and sense of responsibility and self-reliance has been destroyed by the very generous welfare benefits thrown at them by white Australian society as some form of compensation for stealing the country from their ancestors. However great the historic injustices inflicted on aborigines, the current policy, which has turned whole communities into benefit junkies reliant on the state, has done far more harm than good, leading to high unemployment and alcoholism. The policy continued for a long time, supported by political correctness, with opponents routinely denounced for racism. Only recently have the failures of the policy become widely accepted, not least among aboriginal leaders themselves—but only after severe damage has been done.

Political correctness encourages the black community to blame racism by teachers for the underachievement of black boys in schools, rather than tackle the 'all gold chains and no brains' (as Trevor Phillips, the chairman of the Commission for Racial Equality, called it) culture of underachievement that many leading black educationalists believe is the true cause of failure. It is notable that many of the most successful blacks in Britain are from Ghanaian families, who tend to stress traditional values of the importance of education, achievement and self-respect, rather than inculcating a pervasive sense of victimhood. Condoleezza Rice did not rise from poverty in segregated Alabama to become both the most powerful black person and one of the most powerful women in the world by blaming others for her problems (although she would have had much right to), but by hard work, self-discipline and taking responsibility for her own life. If she had concentrated instead on telling the world how hard it is to be a black woman, she almost certainly would not have become the US's first black woman Secretary of State.

In the US, the widespread use of historical slavery as an excuse for failure merely inculcates a defeatist sense of victimhood that may be emotionally comforting in the short term, but does nothing to help African Americans take what steps they can to improve their own lives. As one black New York comedian joked to me: 'I just hate people who use slavery as a crutch.'

The most successful blind person in Britain, the former Home Secretary David Blunkett, achieved cabinet position by overcoming his blindness, rather than eliciting sympathy by succumbing to it.

Persistently blaming the West for many of the Third World's problems discourages Third World countries from facing up to the fact that many, and perhaps most, of their problems are self-inflicted. As China, India, South Korea, Taiwan, Thailand and Malaysia have shown, the key to development is largely in a country's own hands. The world's most failing countries, in the Arab world and Africa, are the ones that most blatantly avoid their own responsibility for their plight by blaming it on the West.

Development aid has a poor record of promoting economic development, and often inculcates cultures of corruption and dependency among governments. Writing off Third World debt can cause a 'moral hazard' that encourages excessive and irresponsible borrowing by governments. Stressing the importance of aid and debt relief may reduce Western guilt, but risks diverting attention from the more important hindrances to development, which in the long run are bad governance, lack of rule of law, corruption, poor education, poor healthcare, excessive bureaucracy, socialism and distorted international trade laws.

The War against Freedom of Speech

The most worrying aspect of political correctness is its success in stifling opposing beliefs.

At its most basic, the censorship is self-imposed. Political correctness succeeds by attaching a sense of moral superiority to itself, and a sense of shame to opposing beliefs. This sense of shame becomes internalised, so that people feel ashamed if they publicly state politically incorrect beliefs, even if they believe them.

Likewise, people feel morally superior opposing political incorrectness, and so feel righteousness in trying to silence the politically incorrect. While the politically incorrect preface themselves with: 'I know I shouldn't say this, but...', the politically correct respond: 'You shouldn't say that!' The politically correct enforce the censorship with powerfully silencing accusations of 'sexism', 'homophobia', 'racism' and 'fascism'. They are widely inappropriately applied, because the aim is not an accurate analysis, but merely to silence opposing views.

The politically correct have long pursued 'no platform' policies for those they disagree with, from universities to national TV. Style guides have been introduced for civil servants, police officers and journalists to weed out unacceptable patterns of speech and use of language. University grant-givers, notably the Economic and Social Research Council, support an almost entirely politically-correct agenda, creating an academic body of work that reinforces politically correct belief. An academic is far more likely to get funding for a project aimed at promoting the benefits of immigration, rather than one wanting to honestly examine its problems.

Even when men were overwhelmingly underachieving compared with women at all levels of the education system, and were twice as likely to be unemployed, three times as likely to commit suicide, three times as likely to be a victim of violent crime, four times as likely to be a drug addict, three times as likely to be alcoholic and nine times as likely to be homeless, the Economic and Social Research Council was still almost exclusively funding work that looked at the problems faced by women. Although men surpass women at almost every measure of social failure, admitting that men also have serious problems simply doesn't fit the politically correct paradigm, and all such research was avoided until it became impossible to deny the 'crisis of masculinity' any longer. University research departments that are meant to extend human understanding end up merely buttressing pre-held beliefs.

One tactic of political correctness is to follow the Orwellian Newspeak approach of trying to eliminate thoughts by eliminating the words, or even unintended associations. Handicapped turns to disabled, black market to shadow market. Many such 'politically correct' language changes merely reflect social changes. Others, however, reflect the determination to find offence where there is none, leading to a semantic wild goose chase, whereby Negro is replaced by Black is replaced by African American is replaced by Person of Colour is replaced by...

Codes of conduct are also used to uphold politically-correct beliefs. Newspapers are bound not to mention the race of a criminal on the grounds that it is 'irrelevant', although they are not banned from mentioning equally irrelevant facts like age, height, or favourite hobbies, and they are not banned from mentioning 'irrelevant' facts such as race when it applies to the Asian business awards, Britain's Black History Month, Halle Berry winning an Oscar or Paul Boateng becoming a cabinet minister.

The politically correct strive to uphold their values by getting those who break them sacked. There are countless examples, with just two of the most high profile being Ray Honeyford, the Bradford head teacher, who was sacked for saying British Asian children should learn English (which is now government policy), and the TV presenter Robert Kilroy-Silk. The demands that the politically incorrect be sacked succeed because of the fear of 'guilt by association', which stops many sympathisers of the offender publicly offering support.

The politically correct belief in censorship can run so deep that the politically correct sometimes justify murder and incitement to murder as a way of suppressing freedom of speech. Many on the left in Britain supported the Ayatollah of Iran's call to murder Salman Rushdie for insulting Islam, and some suggested that the Dutch film maker Theo van Gogh deserved to be killed by an Islamic radical because he was so offensive about Islam.

Even in Western countries with a tradition of freedom of speech, laws have been introduced to curb people saying politically incorrect things. In the Netherlands, a man was jailed for saying 'the Netherlands was full' (an eminently sensible thing to say of Europe's most densely populated country, which has virtually no unspoilt countryside left) on the grounds that it was inciting racial hatred. France has laws criminalising insulting vulnerable minorities such as homosexuals and Muslims (leading to the prosecution of the novelist Michel Houellebecq for saying Islam was 'stupid' in an interview). In Britain there are laws for inciting racial hatred (which for some reason don't apply to Michael Moore's book *Stupid White Men*, even though it clearly incites hatred against whites), and at the time of writing the Labour government are copying an Australian law to criminalise inciting religious hatred, which its advocates hope will curb criticism of Islam.

Free speech is never an absolute. From a gang boss saying 'kill him', to a passenger shouting 'I've got a bomb' on a plane, the freedom to say something cannot be free from responsibility for the consequences. Speech should be curtailed only if it is intended AND likely to cause physical violence, or gravely threatens national security, but political correctness has moved the limitations on free speech beyond that. It has started criminalising speech that merely causes offence, or incites not violence but an emotion (hatred).

The effect is to curb sensitive debates, and to tie police up in countless investigations of commentators. Ann Robinson was investigated for asking what the point of the Welsh was, Robin Page (former presenter of the BBC TV programme *One Man and His Dog*) was arrested overnight for saying he thought countryfolk should have the same rights as other minorities, and Taki was investigated by the Metropolitan Police for insulting black criminals in the *Spectator*.

A country that has long prided itself on its freedom of speech has been reduced by political correctness to a country where, despite endemic levels of violent crime, police spend time investigating and arresting leading writers and broadcasters for what they write and say.

Although political correctness has led to widespread 'speech crimes', it often drifts into the Orwellian 'thought crimes'. Members of the British National Party, a legal democratic political party, have been banned from being civil servants, and can be banned from membership of trade unions. The BNP is odious (as I have written many times), but a civil servant being sacked for being a member of the BNP is being sacked not for anything they have done or even said, but presumed to think.

The creation of 'thought crimes' became almost self-parodic when the *Guardian* trumpeted a machine that could detect whether or not police recruits had racist thoughts. Police racism is damaging to individuals and society, but these recruits would be barred from entering the force not for what they actually say or do, but because of what an electric machine believes they think. George Orwell, where are you?

The politically correct have been highly successful in curbing free speech despite the overwhelming historical evidence that a successful, modern, democratic society can only be built on free speech, when public differences of opinion are fought over with words rather than police investigations. In many ways it is an indictment of the politically correct: if they were more confident of their arguments, they wouldn't be so frightened of debate.

The fear of open public debate about 'their territory' was shown by the *Independent* newspaper's response to the launch of Migrationwatch. Rather than welcoming a group that might balance the very one-sided public debate, the *Independent* said it was a nasty group that 'deserved to close'.

Commenting on the Blair government's attempt to win Muslim votes by criminalising incitement to religious hatred, which Muslim leaders hope will criminalise criticism of Islam, Salman Rushdie wrote:

> To me it is merely further evidence that in Britain, just as in the
> United States, we may need to fight the battle for the
> Enlightenment all over again. That battle, you may remember, was
> about the church's desire to place limits on thought. Diderot's
> novel *La Religieuse*, with its portrayal of nuns and their behavior,

was deliberately blasphemous: It challenged religious authority, with its indexes and inquisitions, on what was possible to say. Most of our contemporary ideas about freedom of speech and imagination come from the Enlightenment. But although we may have thought the battle long since won, if we aren't careful, it is about to be 'un-won'.[4]

So far has the concept of freedom of speech been forgotten, that the words of John Stuart Mill from a hundred and fifty years ago have a sobering effect on the modern mind:

> The time, it is to be hoped, is gone by, when any defence would be necessary of the 'liberty of the press' as one of the securities against corrupt or tyrannical government. No argument, we may suppose, can now be needed, against permitting a legislature or an executive, not identified in interest with the people, to prescribe opinions to them, and determine what doctrines or what arguments they shall be allowed to hear.[5]

Inability to Confront Problems

The stifling of public debate, the preference for emotional comfort over reason, and for political correctness over factual correctness, can often make it very difficult for policy makers to deal with growing problems. The widespread systematic abuse of the asylum system by people smugglers was not confronted for many years after it became obvious because political correctness made it almost impossible for politicians to be honest about the problem. Rather than helping ethnic minorities, political correctness resulted in a notable deterioration in race relations in Britain.

The same applies to the heterosexual HIV epidemic that is being imported to Britain by African immigration, tripling the rate of HIV. For a long time, the issue was not addressed because doctors found it too difficult to talk about. Government epidemiologists and ministers buried their heads for as long as possible, because it was the easiest thing to do, with the government employing a Kenyan epidemiologist to be their spokesman on the issue to avoid accusations of racism. Despite a government inquiry warning of the explosive scale of the problem, and recommending US and Australia-style immigration health tests, the government chose not to act, because, as one cabinet minister said, 'this is not what I entered politics for'.

Other issues that political correctness has made it difficult to confront include the educational failings of boys, and of black boys in particular; female genital mutilation; forced marriages; the growth of unintegrated parallel societies of ethnic minorities; welfare dependency; school discipline; NHS reform; asserting Britain's interest in the European Union; and rising crime, in particular street crime.

Now, one of the biggest issues facing Britain is the rise of radical Islam among Britain's growing Muslim communities. The politically correct response—and that of the British government—is to pander to Islamic militancy by, for example, curbing the freedom to debate Islam, creating tax-funded Islamic schools and campaigning for Muslim Turkey to be admitted as the biggest member of the European Union. The best way to combat Islamic extremism—more free speech—is the one thing that PC undermines.

No country has yet been destroyed by political correctness—although the Netherlands has come close—but the ingredients are there.

Undermining Democracy

Once political correctness becomes hegemonic, the higher up the power and social structure someone is, the more pressure they are under to abide by politically-correct taboos, and the more they will be isolated from their peers if they break them.

As a result, political correctness leads to a huge gulf between elites and commoners, between those who govern and those who are governed.

Although nearly half of the British want to leave the European Union, the fear of being called a little Englander means that not a single Member of Parliament publicly supports withdrawal (although a few do privately). Despite the government's official and the BBC's unofficial policy of promoting mass immigration, opinion polls show 80 per cent of British think there is too much immigration. In almost all western countries, political correctness has undermined democracy's ability to reflect public concern on this issue.

The British public are also generally opposed to multiculturalism, firmly believing that those who come here should try to integrate with British society and culture, rather than isolating themselves in parallel societies. Only recently, after parallel societies started producing murderous terrorists bent on destroying the country, have politicians dared promote the benefits of social cohesion.

Despite tough talking by many governments on the issue of crime, policies over recent decades have generally supported the rights of criminals, whether making it easier for them to avoid being convicted, or emphasising rehabilitation rather than punishment. This has lead to a very low conviction rate, the proliferation of repeat offenders, and absurdities such as burglars having the right to sue householders if they are injured during a burglary.

This emphasis by elites on the rights of criminals is in stark contrast to a public so frustrated with endemic crime that it is overwhelmingly retributive in its attitudes to criminals. When the BBC Today programme held a poll of its readers to choose one policy which a Labour MP Stephen Pound said he would adopt as a private member's bill, the listeners chose the right of homeowners to use any force to defend their properties when invaded by burglars.

Faced with this political incorrectness, Mr Pound withdrew his offer, declaring: 'The people have spoken, the bastards!'[6]

Being less affected by political correctness, and thus being able to think more logically, the general public are on many issues far wiser than their leaders. Intellectuals are often not wiser than non-intellectuals, just better at sophistry and so better able to create such convincing specious arguments on why black is really white that they believe it themselves.

Just as political correctness's soft opposition to freedom of speech is sometimes hardened into censorship, so political correctness's soft opposition to representative democracy is hardened into outlawing certain political parties.

As mentioned earlier, the Labour government are proscribing membership of the legal democratic party the BNP for certain groups of people such as civil servants, and there are many on the left who want to ban the BNP altogether. Nick Griffin, the BNP leader, was arrested by police in a dawn raid on his Welsh farm on allegations of hate speech.

In Belgium, the Vlaams Blok political party was declared illegal by the Supreme Court for breaching laws against racism, despite the fact that it is the most popular political party in the Flemish half of the country. In Australia, the leading anti-multiculturalism politician, Pauline Hanson, was imprisoned for her speeches.

The European Union imposed sanctions on Austria, in effect blocking it from taking part in EU politics, when its citizens elected Jorg Haider, the leader of the far-right Freedom Party, to government. Sometimes, the politically correct left take more extreme actions in their determination to prevent democracy—the anti-immigrant politician Pym Fortuyn was murdered by a left-wing animal rights activist to stop him becoming prime minister.

One must be very disillusioned with democracy not to find it at least slightly unsettling that in Europe in the twenty-first century government employees are being banned from joining certain legal political parties but not others, legal democratic party leaders are being arrested in dawn raids for what they have said, and political parties leading the polls are being banned by judges.

As James C. Bennett, the author and fellow of the Hudson Institute, wrote: 'of democracy, immigration and multiculturalism, we must pick from any two'.[7] Which two would you like?

Political Instability

The stifling of freedom of speech, the undermining of democracy by creating a gulf between the ruled and the rulers, and the inability to confront nascent problems are a potent set of ingredients created by political correctness that can lead to political instability even in the most apparently stable countries.

The closing down of political debate does not deal with problems, but allows them to fester and grow. Self-censorship in the media does not stop people seeing things with their own eyes, and talking about them within the privacy of their own homes. If mainstream parties don't address public concern, extremist parties, not worried about the pariah status of being politically incorrect, will step into the vacuum between the ruled and the rulers. Banning extremist political parties does not deal with public concern, but merely suppresses the political expression of it.

The closing down of normal democratic pressure valves can lead to explosive tensions in society, as the Netherlands most spectacularly found with the phenomenal rise and assassination of Pim Fortuyn. After his death, his party, Fortuyn's List, smashed the cosy consensual politics of the country which had determinedly blocked all discussion of the effects of mass immigration, and soon almost all mainstream parties, including those on the left, adopted his policies. Within two years, the Islam critic and film-maker Theo van Gogh was murdered by an Islamic extremist in the Netherlands, prompting a wave of religious violence that saw mosques, churches and schools burnt down. The Netherlands has been turned from one of the most socially cohesive countries in the world, where the prime minister could ride a bicycle in public, to one where Muslim and non-Muslim communities live in fear of each other.

In the Netherlands, political correctness undermined the functioning of its liberal democracy to such an extent that it was no longer able to debate and tackle serious and growing problems until the tensions were so great in society that they exploded. It would have been far better if the problems had been openly discussed and addressed as they arose, diffusing tensions rather than exacerbating them.

Nor is the Netherlands alone. Other countries, such as Denmark, have suffered similar, if smaller scale, political earthquakes. Belgium seems to be heading for a similar political explosion, with the Vlaams Berlang (the relaunched Vlaams Blok after it was banned) growing steadily in popularity on the issues of independence for the Flemish region and immigration.

7

How Political Correctness Affects Policies

Only a brave person is willing to admit honestly, and fearlessly to face, what a sincere and logical mind discovers.

Rodan of Alexandria

Being a way of thinking about policies, rather than a policy in itself, the tentacles of political correctness touch a vast array of issues, from the economics of the NHS to law and order, from the European Union to whaling. All involve received beliefs that are instinctively promoted and counter-beliefs that are silenced. These are just some examples of the policy areas affected by political correctness.

Women's Pay

One of the rallying cries of the politically correct is the 'unacceptable' gender pay gap between men and women: women's full-time hourly pay is on average just 80 per cent of that of men. Unions and the Equal Opportunities Commission regularly launch campaigns on the issue, insisting it shows just how prevalent sex discrimination still is in the workplace. Few ask whether the gender pay gap may be due to other factors, because that would be to appear to justify the pay gap and thus sex discrimination.

It is clear that, other factors being the same, equal pay for equal work is not just fundamentally fair and just, but also an essential basis for an efficient economy taking optimal advantage of the skills of all workers. If women are paid less for equal work than men just because of their gender, then that is irrational, prejudicial and unjust.

But even in a workforce with a total absence of sex discrimination, there could still be a gender pay gap. The presumption that any pay gap is only explicable by sex discrimination is a presumption that men and women are identical in all their lifestyle choices and legal rights, when they are not.

Men's legal retirement age is five years older than women's, encouraging them to work longer careers, which uplifts their average earnings. Women get far more extensive parental leave than men, encouraging career breaks and limiting their lifetime work experience, thus depressing their average wages. On average, each week, men work nearly twice as many hours in paid employment as women, building up considerably more experience in their careers, which in a meritocracy would be reflected in greater pay. In addition, surveys suggest that women opt for more socially rewarding or emotionally fulfilling jobs, while men put a higher priority on high wages at whatever cost.

The danger is that if the only accepted explanation for income differentials is discrimination, then a range of policies will be adopted that may either be counter-productive, or actually introduce discrimination. Policies that specifically favour women at the expense of men are not only unfair, but by undermining meritocracy they undermine the efficiency of the labour market. Any initiative that is being introduced—such as the right for employees to know their colleagues' salaries—would be far less effective at producing the desired outcome than intended, and could ultimately just introduce more red tape, damaging economic efficiency and job creation.

Europe

Those opposed to further transferring of national powers to the European Union, or joining the European single currency, are often denounced as 'Little Englanders'. In an article Chancellor Gordon Brown rehearsed a whole series of problems with the European economy and why Britain should not join the Euro, and then said, without any obvious irony, that 'pro-Europeans' such as himself had to combat anti-European 'prejudice'. The clear suggestion was that opposition to further European integration could only be explicable by prejudice, presumably a dislike of Europeans.

Reports from politically correct media such as the BBC and the *Guardian* are underlined by a firm belief that being 'pro-European' is modern, cosmopolitan and progressive, and that to be 'anti-European' is to be a Little Englander, xenophobic, living in the past and obsessed by the Second World War. The former Europe minister Denis MacShane said explicitly that eurosceptics were driven by xenophobia.

But the arguments about centralisation or decentralisation of powers permeate all political entities from the United States to Britain to London. Arguing that no more powers in certain policy areas—such as working hours—should be transferred from London to Brussels is not necessarily being a Little Englander any more than arguing that powers shouldn't be transferred from Sacramento to Washington is being a Little Californian, or arguing that some policies are best formulated in Edinburgh rather than Westminster is being a Little Scot.

The optimal balance of power between centre and regions has to be found for all levels. There is a contradiction between the politically correct presumption at the national level that powers should be transferred downwards (i.e. devolved to the regions), but that at the continental level they should be transferred upwards (i.e. devolved to Brussels).

There are many reasons to be opposed to further political integration in Europe, which can have more to do with a belief in accountability and keeping democratic decision making as close to the *demos* as practicably possible. There are profound economic arguments against joining the euro, shared by many of Britain's top economists, that have nothing to do with prejudice.

Capitalism

Few things have done more in the history of humanity to improve human existence than capitalism. It has created wealth at an unprecedented pace, eliminated poverty, abolished hunger, improved housing, and increased life expectancy. It created the wealth so that people could enjoy holidays and it created the drugs to cure diseases. No society on Earth has ever had such a privileged existence as the capitalist West—even the lives of the poorest sections of society are almost immeasurably better in almost all ways than under any other form of economic system.

All alternatives have proved disastrous failures, creating untold human misery. Throughout Eastern Europe, Russia, Cuba, Vietnam and North Korea communism has confined people to poverty and short life expectancy. When the world's two most populous countries, India and China, embraced capitalism, hundreds of millions of people were taken out of poverty.

Anything that has done so much for humanity should be seen as one of the best things that humanity has invented. Yet capitalism has persistently had a bad name: political correctness decrees it a 'bad thing', because it is based on people pursuing their own self interest, and richer people making profits out of poorer people.

But a system has to be judged by its results. Capitalism has proved perfectly able to curb its harsher aspects by creating the wealth to pay for the welfare state, social housing and socialised medicine. Capitalist societies have done far more to preserve their natural resources than any other non-primitive societies.

Political correctness causes widespread unease with capitalism, which makes governments less likely to pursue capitalist alternatives to established policies in various areas, such as health and education, as would be the case if their only concern were maximising the benefits to society.

The National Health Service

The NHS is one of the few organisations that actually runs on the principle of political correctness, or as its founder Aneurin Bevan stated, on an ethical principle. Until recently, political correctness silenced any non-academic debate about alternatives to a free-at-the-point-of-use, taxpayer-funded, state-owned monopoly. However, there is overwhelming evidence that the NHS system delivers worse health outcomes for all categories of patient, and is more unequal, than many other health systems, such as social insurance with mixed public and private provision. The argument on this has been moving in Britain, and may finally lead to a better NHS, but in the meantime political correctness is literally killing people.

Crime and Punishment

The politically correct have a particular problem with crime. Their instinct is to support the criminal rather the victim of their crime, because criminals tend to be more socially disadvantaged and poorer, and their victims more privileged and richer.

The purpose of all law and order policies is to provide justice (otherwise known as retribution), deterrence and rehabilitation. But because of the growing politically correct concern for the socially disadvantaged perpetrators of crime, rather than for the privileged victims of it, policies have tended increasingly to emphasise rehabilitation over retribution, with a greater emphasis on the rights of suspected and proven criminals, and less on the rights of actual or potential victims.

There has been huge public outrage at the logical extension of this, with prosecutions of people who are defending their properties from criminals, rather than the criminals who are attacking them.

Much to the distress of the politically correct, prison numbers in the UK are at record level, but are in fact far lower than if the number of inmates had followed the rise in the number of criminals. Charles Murray, the American academic, has calculated that if Britain in 2004 jailed the same ratio of people relative to the number of the most serious offences that it imprisoned in 1954, the prison population would be around 300,000, more than 200,000 above the real level.

According to Murray, in 1954 for every three robbers convicted, one was sent to jail, a ratio of 1:3. By 2002, this ratio was 1:22. For burglars, the ratio was 1:18 in 1954 compared with 1:59 in 2002, while for serious wounding the ratio was 1:5 in 1954 compared with 1:12 in 2002. In other words, the chance of being jailed for committing a crime is between a half and one-seventh of what it was half a century ago. The rise in crime over the last 50 years has matched the decline in chance of being sent to prison.

Obviously prison is far from perfect, and re-offending rates remain high. But there is abundant evidence that prison actually works in reducing crime, by several measurements. The shrinking risk of being sent to prison has reduced the deterrence of prison, and made committing crime far more attractive by tipping the balance from risk to reward. People in prison are also simply unable to commit crimes while inside. Political correctness has tipped the balance from the victim of crime to the perpetrators of crime, and society has paid with the inevitable result—an increase in crime. Many criminals have also paid because they were drawn into a criminal lifestyle whereas under a non-PC system they would have remained law-abiding citizens, not daring to stray.

Environmental Protection

The environmental movement has been one of the most successful mass movements of all time, second only perhaps to women's rights. From the 1970s onwards, it highlighted valid concerns about environmental degradation, put it on the political agenda, confronted vested interests, won the main intellectual arguments, and was the driving force behind the dramatic change in attitudes and legislation, as least in the western industrialised world.

But a politically correct paradigm was created in which the world's environment was presumed to be going to hell in a handcart—total destruction of the rainforests, the extinction of many if not most species, acid rain, the destruction of the ozone layer, the world was set to freeze until it was believed the world was set to boil. Good environmental news was suppressed because it didn't fit this paradigm, bad news, however shakily founded, was trumpeted, and those who questioned it were vilified. In this atmosphere, politicians in most of the West, and certainly the UK, could only say they would side with the environmentalists, promising ever greater environmental protection.

But the environmental movement in the West has become the victim of its own extraordinary success. In the UK, the rivers are cleaner than they have been since before the industrial revolution, the air in London is the cleanest it has been for over 300 years and forest cover is the highest it has been for more than 200 years, even if you discount monocultural conifer plantations. Rather than species becoming extinct, previously nationally extinct species are being reintroduced from other parts of the world, and endangered species such as otters and wild boars are thriving. Acid rain is no longer a problem, and the ozone layer is healing itself after suitable action was taken. Global warming is, however, still a threat.

Human Rights Abuses

Political correctness has ensured that in the West the severity of the human rights abuse depends more on who is abusing and who is abused than it does on the actual abuse. Western governments making small scale abuses are criticised far more harshly than the governments of third-world countries who are responsible for the overwhelming majority and most extreme examples of human rights abuses in the world. In its 2004 annual report, the human rights organisation Amnesty International showed it had succumbed to fashionable political correctness by declaring that the US has done more damage to human rights than any other country in the last 50 years, somehow ignoring Pol Pot's Kampuchea, Mao Zedong's China, Kim Il Sung's North Korea, let alone the extreme human rights violations in countries such as Saudi Arabia, Algeria, Burma, Rwanda or Sudan.

Abuse is abhorrent irrespective of who is doing the abuse, and a champion of human rights must be unequivocal and impartial in its condemnation of abuses, rather than following a fashionable politically correct agenda of only attacking small scale abuses by western governments and ignoring the vastly greater abuses by non-western governments. Otherwise, there is a danger of implicitly condoning the human rights abuses of developing nations.

Racial Profiling

Racial profiling—the use of ethnic characteristics in detecting criminals—has become taboo in the UK, but more as a result of political correctness than the result of any rational argument.

Asked if racial profiling was ever justified, James Q. Wilson, the celebrated American criminologist, said in an interview:

If by racial profiling you mean the police stopping or arresting somebody because of their racial identity, the answer is no; it ought to be illegal. If you mean whether race may be a factor in deciding whether a person should be a suspect, the answer is, under many circumstances it is properly taken as a factor. If you are in a white neighbourhood and a burglary is reported, and you see a young black man walking down the street at 2:00 a.m., are you more likely to stop him than if you see a young white man walking down the street? Of course, because you say to yourself the first is less likely to be here naturally than the latter. I don't think you can eliminate race entirely from police judgments any more than you can eliminate gender. Men are many times more likely to be violent and to commit crimes than women. So if you see a man and a woman walking down the street right after a burglary at 2:00 a.m., are you more likely to stop the man or the woman? More likely to stop the man.[1]

As well as racial and gender profiling, there is also age-profiling, with police far more likely to stop someone for robbery if they are under 30 than over 60, on the simple basis that the young are far more likely to commit certain crimes than the old. If, as Home Office figures suggest, Afro-Caribbean men are around ten times more likely to commit violent street crimes than white men, then it is not a reflection of police prejudice but a reflection of relative crime rates if Afro-Caribbeans are investigated for violent street crimes proportionately more frequently than whites.

The most extreme example of police profiling is the one used in the battle against large-scale terrorism. Islamic groups in Britain have complained that they been unfairly targeted by the raft of anti-terrorism legislation that has been brought in since the attacks in New York on September 11th 2001. They have backed up their complaints of discrimination and racial profiling with statistics showing that almost all the people investigated under this legislation were Muslims. Few things show more clearly the flaws in politically correct analysis than the fact that the *Guardian* newspaper treated the complaints so uncritically that it carried them in a splash story on its front page.

The simple fact, awkward as it is for the politically correct, is that Britain doesn't face the threat of mass terrorism from militant Hindus. Britain faces a very significant threat of a large-scale terrorist attack perpetuated by Muslims in the name of Islam, but an insignificant threat of terrorism from any other religious group (even Northern Irish Catholics by comparison).

The demand that police fighting mass terrorism should investigate all religious groups equally is in fact a demand that the police investigate thousands of people they know to be totally innocent so as not to cause offence to Muslims. Not only would this be an extraordinary waste of police resources, hampering their ability to tackle terrorism, but it would be an infringement of the rights of other religious groups not to be investigated without any grounds of suspicion.

The reason that there is a taboo about racial profiling and yet complete acceptance of gender and age profiling has nothing to do with any rational argument about law enforcement, but rather about the political correctness which makes it unacceptable to target vulnerable groups such as Afro-Caribbeans and Muslims, but perfectly acceptable to target non-vulnerable groups such as men.

Excessive racial profiling—up to and including, as James Q. Wilson mentioned, stopping people just because of their ethnicity without any other cause for suspicion— can indeed cause justifiable anger and alienation in some communities, which could itself prove counterproductive. The police must strike a balance between policing efficiency and offending minorities.

8

The Trouble with Discrimination

Once upon a time, 'discrimination'—which is so central to much of political correctness it is worth special consideration—was seen as a positive attribute, which enabled people to discriminate between good and bad. People of discernment actually tried to educate themselves to become 'discriminating', a by-word for having good judgement.

Now 'discrimination'—an ill-defined, catch-all term—has become one of the most unforgivable sins, something that no respectable person would seek to justify under any circumstances. Anything that is portrayed as 'discriminatory' in any way is automatically deemed intolerable.

The fight against discrimination is one of the foundation stones of political correctness, underpinning and motivating much of it. Shami Chakrabarti, on becoming director of the left-wing pressure group Liberty, declared she believed in 'zero tolerance of any form of discrimination'. The European Charter of Fundamental Rights promises to outlaw all discrimination, turning politically correct sloganeering into Europe-wide law upheld by a court in Luxembourg:

> Any discrimination based on any ground such as sex, race, colour, ethnic or social origin, genetic features, language, religion or belief, political or any other opinion, membership of a national minority, property, birth, disability, age or sexual orientation shall be prohibited.

There are noble intentions behind these declarations that few civilised people would disagree with, and making these declarations rewards the declarers by making them feel virtuous (as one government lawyer said to me). The fight against discrimination has righted many hideous wrongs, such as denial of services to ethnic minorities and women's disenfrashisement. But having won the most obvious and justifiable battles, the intentions are often rendered meaningless by the flawed, often hypocritical and usually intolerant thinking behind them.

Political correctness constricts people's range of thought to such a degree that a rational public discussion on discrimination has become almost impossible, and it usually descends into learnt ritual denunciations of anyone going against the received text. Anyone who supports discrimination, either explicit or implicit, is vilified. After all, how could any decent person speak out in favour of discrimination?

Well, supporters of positive discrimination, for starters.

Discrimination is highly complex phenomenon that has both positive and negative aspects, and while its negative manifestations can be very damaging and should be fought against, some forms of discrimination are also essential for the operation of society. Many forms of discrimination are widely accepted and unquestioned simply because of the benefits that they bring. It would be very difficult to prevent roads becoming far more dangerous than they already are if licensing authorities were not allowed to indulge in age discrimination both in awarding driving licences in the first place, and then in determining who should be required to have re-testing on age grounds.

It is important to distinguish between two forms of discrimination, which we can call rational and irrational. Rational discrimination is the attribution to individuals of the known average characteristics of a group to which they belong. Young men pay higher rates for car insurance than young women and older men, because young men are, on average, more dangerous drivers than young women and older men. A young man who is a safe driver is thus discriminated against because of the characteristics of other people in his age and sex group.

By contrast, irrational discrimination is just prejudice that is not based on evidence. Until very recently women were discouraged from being doctors on the grounds they did not make good doctors, even though they make just as good (and perhaps in some ways better) doctors than men. Not employing an otherwise perfectly qualified person as an accountant just because they are gay or black is simply irrational prejudicial discrimination.

Sometimes discrimination is a mixture of rational and irrational. The campaign among some feminists to ban all men from working with primary school children is partly based on the fact that men are more likely to sexually abuse children than women, and partly on prejudice against men.

Irrational, prejudicial discrimination is unjust, damaging both societies and individuals. However, rational discrimination is far more complex. Although it may be unfair on some individuals, rational discrimination is often not just accepted, but used as a basis of policy, because there are wider social benefits and any alternatives have even greater drawbacks.

Those who campaign against ageism are unlikely to campaign for the abolition of the age of consent on the grounds that it discriminates against children, making them unable to enjoy legal sex simply because of their age. Some 15 year olds are mature enough to enjoy healthy sexual relationships, but it is near impossible for the law to judge between those who are mature enough and those that aren't, so blanket age discrimination is used.

Those who declare that all forms of discrimination are intolerable are unlikely to campaign for 12-year-olds to be allowed to vote or buy cigarettes and alcohol. They are unlikely to demand that pension companies and health insurers should be banned from taking age into account, when setting premiums and annuities, an act that would make those industries financially unviable. They are

71

unlikely to campaign against free bus passes for those of pensionable age, a clear example of age discrimination. A poor 59-year-old man is far more deserving of a free bus pass than a 70-year-old millionaire, and yet is discriminated against because of his age.

Anti-discrimination campaigners may publicly declare that all discrimination on the grounds of sex should be outlawed, but they are unlikely to agree that all men should have the right to use women's toilets, that men should be allowed to go to women's gyms, or to demand overturning the right of women's clothes shops to refuse to employ men.

The European Charter of Fundamental Rights prohibits discrimination on the grounds of 'language', but insisting that nurses can speak English and don't need an interpreter when applying for a job in the NHS is pure linguistic discrimination which is accepted because the alternative would be very impractical and costly.

All countries practice discrimination on the grounds of national origin when it comes to immigration, because anything else is unworkable. All citizens of EU countries have the automatic right to live and work in the UK, but not citizens of American, Asian or African countries. US citizens can visit the UK without a visa, but Nigerian and Indian citizens cannot. The reason quite simply is that the proportion of Americans who don't return and then break immigration law is very low, while the proportion of Nigerians and Indians is high. The government tracks records of immigration law infringement by national origin, and slaps entry visas on those nations where infringement rates are high. A rich Indian businessman is required to get a visa even though he is less likely to become a burden on the state or break immigration laws than a poor American, who doesn't need a visa. The Indian is being discriminated against on the basis of national origin, unjustly affected by the high infringement rates of his co-nationals. It is blatant discrimination, but every country in the world employs such discrimination because no country has managed to find a workable non-discriminatory system.

Rational discrimination does create victims, and sometimes it can—and should—be avoided. In all cases a balance has to be made between the social divisiveness of accepting rational discrimination, and the drawbacks of avoiding it.

Men, on average, make better firefighters than women, because firefighting requires physical strength and men are stronger on average than women. But the old blanket ban on women becoming firefighters was a blunt and unnecessary form of rational discrimination, since it is easy as part of the assessment procedure to assess the relevant characteristic, strength, rather than the ultimately irrelevant one, gender.

In other instances, rational discrimination is almost impossible to avoid. One sixteen-year-old may be an innately safer driver than another eighteen-year-old, but is denied a provisional licence purely because of her age. Any driving licence system that doesn't use age discrimination would have to have some form of pre-testing for suitability to be allowed behind the wheel of a car, which would be costly, inefficient and ineffective compared with blanket age discrimination.

The pension and insurance industries are ubiquitous users of age and sexual discrimination, rationally calculated in their actuarial tables. Men pay smaller pension contributions than women for a given level of private pension, for the simple reason that, on average, they have shorter lives and so on average claim less. Old people pay more for private health insurance than young people, because on average they are likely to make more claims. This form of rational age and sex discrimination is accepted because it causes little social division.

However, pension and insurance companies would also be capable of using race to determine premiums, because the actuarial information is available. Ethnic minorities in the UK have a much shorter life expectancy than whites, and so, according to actuarial tables, they should pay less for private pensions. In contrast, because they tend to live in higher crime neighbourhoods, they tend to be greater victims of car crime, and according to the cold arithmetic of the actuaries, they would be charged higher car insurance premiums to reflect that risk. However, although age and sex discrimination is accepted in the provision of financial services, race discrimination isn't because, although it could be justified by the actuaries, it is far more socially divisive. Asking someone their race to determine their cost of car insurance or pension contributions would be redolent of apartheid. (Although the PC may just accept an insurance firm using black people's shorter life expectancies to offer them lower pension contributions, it would set a terrible precedent.)

The various forms of rational discrimination that are widely accepted are not often called discrimination— although that is clearly what they are—because accepting that some discrimination is actually essential to the working of a society would undermine the public acceptance of 'zero tolerance of all forms of discrimination'. The war on discrimination would become meaningless if there were general public awareness that actually some forms of discrimination are needed.

Double Standards on Discrimination

There are widespread double standards on various forms of discrimination. In general, discrimination—even irrational, prejudicial discrimination—is either tolerated or promoted so long as it is against the powerful, while discrimination against those deemed vulnerable is deemed indefensible. 'Gender profiling' by police forces that targets men is perfectly acceptable, while 'racial profiling' which targets blacks is not (see chapter 7).

Those who wage war on 'all forms of discrimination' often promote so-called 'positive discrimination', which is nonetheless discrimination which should thus supposedly be worthy of 'zero tolerance'.

The difference in retirement age between men and women is irrational prejudicial discrimination, the continuation of which (at least until 2020) is only explicable because it is men (otherwise perceived to be privileged) who are discriminated against. It is inconceivable that if it were women who were discriminated against that it would not have ended by now, even though it would be slightly more justifiable because women actually live longer.

There are no longer any male-only colleges in Oxford and Cambridge, having come under great pressure to change. But women-only colleges, which are just as blatantly sexist, continue to justify their existence on the grounds that they benefit women—despite the fact that women greatly outperform men at all levels of the education system, up to and including the attainment of first-class university degrees.

Women in the UK get far more generous parental leave than men, a legalised form of sex discrimination that is not entirely justified by biology, as Scandinavian countries have shown. Women adopting babies have demanded the same maternity rights as women who have babies, arguing that babies who are adopted should not be discriminated against in terms of their rights to maternal care. But then there would be absolutely no grounds other than simple sex discrimination to deny men who adopt babies the same parental leave rights as women who adopt babies. If men who adopt babies are given the same rights as women who adopt babies, who are themselves given the same rights as women who give birth to babies, you end up in the absurd position that men who adopt babies have far better parental leave than men who father their own babies.

Discrimination on the grounds of religion is meant to be barred, but there are many charity groups that offer help specifically on the basis of someone's religion, noticeably Jews or Muslims. In contrast, charities such as Christian Aid give most of their aid to non-Christians.

Discrimination on the grounds of race is supposed to be barred, unless it is for training schemes open only to ethnic minorities, or in admission to US universities, where whites—even those from poor, deprived back-grounds—are openly discriminated against purely on the basis of skin colour by being automatically awarded fewer points as part of the entry assessment.

The Black Police Association gets around the inherent racism of its membership criteria by saying that it is open to anyone who has experience of racism whatever their ethnic background—it has many north Africans who are virtually identical to British whites—but it is not open to Jews or Irish, despite the existence of anti-Semitism and anti-Irish prejudice. (In effect, the Black Police Association has a sign on its doors saying: 'no Jews or Irish'.)

The 'white Australia' immigration policy of the 1960s was internationally condemned until it was abandoned, but there have been no international protests in the last few years about India offering citizenship to any of the 20 million people of Indian ethnic origin not living in India (whether or not they have Indian parents, have ever been to India, practice any Indian religion or speak any Indian language), or about Ghana offering an automatic right of residency to any blacks who live in the West (whether or not their ancestors came from Ghana), but not any whites or Asians. The disparity in reactions to Australia's policy and India's and Ghana's is only explicable by political correctness.

There have been many public complaints about sports competitions (such as Wimbledon tennis) having higher value prizes for men rather than women. But the demands for gender-blindness in the prizes don't extend to the tournaments themselves, which are still divided between men's and women's competition. Logically, if the prize doesn't discriminate between men and women, then the competition that leads to those prizes shouldn't either. But there is remarkably little demand for women to be allowed to enter men's competitions or visa versa (i.e. just let the best person win, whether man or woman) because few women would ever win anything at all. The demand for equal treatment only goes as far is it advantages what is deemed the less privileged sex. Those who insist on equal prizes, because anything else is discrimination, should explain why it is not discrimination for men to be denied an equal right to compete for the women's prize. If there really were zero tolerance of sex discrimination in sport— as opposed to selective discrimination—then women would win virtually nothing.

The existence of women's tournaments and the nearly equal prize money for them is already a form of positive discrimination that gives to women tennis players the chance to win money that would be unavailable to them if there really were no sex discrimination in tennis.

Although it may be good to create separate games for women, because then at least they might have a chance of winning, it would be unthinkable to make the same case for creating a 'whites only' world athletics championship. Black athletes dominate many events. White men, for example, very rarely win the 100 metres in the Olympics. It is currently just as pointless being a white 100-metre sprinter in colour-blind sporting competitions as it would be being a women 100-metre sprinter in gender-blind sporting competitions.

It is clear that discrimination itself is usually not the problem, but the effect that such discrimination has. The war on discrimination is often little more than a war on privilege (whether earned or unearned), but a war that dare not declare its name: if it were seen to be a war on privilege it would never be able to command the overwhelming public support that the war on discrimination has. People tend not to support attacks on privilege because they aspire to privilege, but they strongly support 'fair play'.

9

The Dissidents from Political Correctness

It is necessary to the happiness of man that he be mentally faithful to himself.

Tom Paine, 'The Age of Reason'

My message to the media is: Wake up! The silencing of authentic debate among feminists just helps the rise of the far Right. When the media get locked in their Northeastern ghetto and become slaves of the feminist establishment and fanatical special interests, the American audience ends up looking to conservative voices for common sense. As a libertarian Democrat, I protest against this self-defeating tyranny of political correctness.

Camille Paglia, 'Vamps and Tramps'

An apparent paradox of political correctness is that, like advertising, virtually everyone denies being affected by it, but in fact virtually everyone is.

Political correctness is a way of thinking—or rather emoting—that often so engulfs someone's mind that they are unaware of it. If you wear rose-tinted glasses long enough, it seems normal that the whole world is rose.

Some people, notably most of humanity outside the Western world, have not been inflicted with political correctness. Others remain unable to see beyond it for their entire lives.

Some in the West are little afflicted by political correctness, often becoming thorns in the side of the left-wing establishment, and personally targeted because of their dissention. Notable figures include the philosopher Roger Scruton (who long warned against multiculturalism and the erosion of the nation state), the US scholar Charles Murray (who writes on the impact of group differences on policy, and retributive justice), the authors Frederick Forsyth and V.S. Naipaul (both opposed to multiculturalism), and the former chief inspector of schools Chris Woodhead (who has thundered against PC educational nostrums).

Those most zealously opposed to PC tend to be those who were once infected by it and then broke free. Like Winston Smith in George Orwell's *1984*, the doubts often start slowly at first, with people realising the little lies and distortions. First they justify them as white lies, excusing them as being for the greater good. But as they start thinking about the lies, they start realising how prolific they are, and start wondering about the truth they conceal. Eventually, they become convinced that you cannot reach the truth through telling lies, and that, as the Bible said— in a rather different context—'the truth shall make you free'.

The pieces fall into place, and a new picture of the world-view emerges. The PC way of thinking is replaced with a new way of thinking—or rather an old one—that puts the emphasis on factual correctness rather than political correctness, and on reason rather than emotion. They are, in the classic definition of neo-conservatives, 'liberals mugged by reality', but often still liberal in the classical sense.

Those who journey from political correctness to truth often risk public disapprobation, but it is notable that most never lose their tolerance or humanity, and retain their fundamental values. They may question the politics of race, but not that racism is bad; they may question campaigns about women's pay, but not that women and men deserve equality of treatment; they may realise that western civilisation—with its extraordinary ability to create wealth and culture while promoting freedom, equality, and democracy—is, by almost all measures, the best civilisation that humanity has yet created, but that doesn't make them Islamophobes.

In the US, becoming a dissident of left-wing political correctness has almost turned into a literary genre in itself. Countless books denounce the effects of PC in universities, the media and politics.

One of the most high profile defectors from political to factual correctness is David Horowitz, who for many years was a leading (far) left commentator, who had 'second thoughts' after a friend was murdered by the Black Panthers. He has now become a scourge of the dishonesty of the left and political correctness. One of his books, *Left Illusions: An Intellectual Odyssey,* contains the essay 'The Era of Progressive Witch-Hunts' in which he argues that the rise of politically correct witch-hunts in recent years and other forms of behavioural policing have 'been far worse in... consequences to individuals and freedom of expression'[1] than the McCarthy witch-hunts'. He also explained the appeal of the politically correct mentality: 'We were partisans of a cause that confirmed our humanity, even as it denied humanity to those who opposed us',[2] and explained that 'hatred of self, and by extension one's country, is the root of the radical cause'.[3]

Another top journalist who tired of the distortions of political correctness was Emmy award-winner Bernard Goldberg, who spent 28 years at CBS television news, only to denounce it—and its famously left-wing presenter Dan Rather—when he retired in the book *Bias: A CBS Insider Exposes How the Media Distort the News.* He details not just the liberal bias that pervades CBS, but how journalists were in hock to victim pressure groups, put 'sensitivity' ahead of 'facts', refused to tell the truth, and indulged in liberal hate-speech—denouncing as 'right-wing' anyone to the right of Lenin.

It is notable in the environmental field how many of those closely involved in it have lost faith in the main tenets of modern environmentalism—which in many ways has become a secular religion.

81

Patrick Moore, a Canadian who was one of the co-founders of Greenpeace, has been demonised as 'Judas' by the environmental movement because he eventually turned into an environmental optimist, loudly critical of the anti-scientific, anti-human scare tactics of the organisation he helped create. Gregg Easterbrook, the former environment correspondent of the *Washington Post*, got so frustrated with the deception of writing almost nothing but gloomy environment stories, that in 1995 he published the book *A Moment on the Earth: the Coming Age of Environmental Optimism* about how the world's environment was actually getting better.

Some years later, the Danish statistician Bjorn Lomborg, a former member of Greenpeace, got a class of his to collect the statistics to confirm what everyone knew, that the environment was getting worse. When, confounding their earlier politically correct certainty, they found that the large majority of statistics pointed the other way, he wrote *The Skeptical Environmentalist*, about how the world's environment is getting better. He was rewarded for his dissidence from the politically correct dogma by a well orchestrated campaign of vilification, denunciation and academic persecution by the environmental movement, including a failed attempt to get him convicted of academic fraud and a pie-throwing attack in a bookshop by the environmental campaigner Mark Lynas, showing his intolerance of intellectual dissent.

Political activists have also turned on political correctness. In the US, the lesbian Tammy Bruce, one-time president of the Los Angeles chapter of the National Organisation of Woman, was once described by Andrea Dworkin as 'a brilliant feminist, activist, and iconoclast'. But she performed a spectacular U-turn, launching powerful attacks on political correctness and the destructive agenda of left-wing elites in two books: *The New Thought Police: Inside the Left's Assault on Free Speech and Free Minds* and *The Death of Right and Wrong: Exposing the*

Left's Assault on Our Culture and Values. In them, she details the rise of 'left-wing McCarthyism' where 'left-wing elites' desperately try to silence their critics rather than engage in debate. She lambastes feminists' hatred of men and marriage, the Black elite's championing of violent rap music, and academia's anti-Americanism, and argues that multiculturalism, identity politics and 'relativism' turned American society into a 'moral vacuum' incapable of distinguishing right from wrong. But, despite all this, she insists she is not a conservative—she is still a lesbian feminist liberal.

10

How Political Correctness can be Defeated

Great is truth, and mighty above all things.

Book of Esdras

I disapprove of what you say, but I will defend to the death your right to say it.

attributed to Voltaire

There is nothing inevitable about the ascendancy of the ideology of political correctness, and indeed there are already chinks in its armour. The main one, mentioned before, is that political correctness has now become almost politically incorrect itself—few will defend it in principle, even though they will fight for it in practice. This unpopularity of political correctness more than anything represents a state of denial, with people not wanting to accept the way their thought processes have been moulded.

As mentioned in chapter 9, the sheer inconsistencies of political correctness, and its conflict with factual correctness, are leading more and more respectable US commentators to turn their guns on it.

Political correctness, as I mentioned in chapter 4, is essentially the product of a powerful but decadent civilisation which feels secure enough to forego reasoning for emoting, and to subjugate truth to goodness. However, the terrorist attacks of September 11th 2001, and those that followed in Bali, Madrid and London, have led to a sense of vulnerability that have made people far more hard-headed about the real benefits and drawbacks of Western civilisation.

In the Netherlands, where multiculturalism has descended into mosque and church burnings, government ministers now admit they 'were naïve' and there is such a backlash that Dutch children are now being taught Dutch history again (previously ditched for being too Dutch-centric). In Britain, and much of the rest of Europe, multiculturalism is taking a severe battering because of the threat it poses to social cohesion, putting its politically correct defenders on the defensive.

In the US, the fear of Islamic terrorism is one of the factors that led to the rightwards political shift that resulted in the Bush re-election in 2004, which is openly challenging many of the nostrums of political correctness.

Although most mainstream media, such as the *New York Times* and CBS, remain unable to break free of political correctness, the new media from talk radio to the internet have broken the media monopoly, allowing the spreading of subversive politically incorrect thoughts. Many blogs specialise in debunking political correctness.

Hollywood, once unable to rise above turning political correctness into pleasing images, has now started broadening its philosophical view. Cult films, such as *South Park*, have long poked fun at political correctness, but now major Hollywood films are sending out unprecedented politically incorrect messages. *Spiderman II* was an allegory on how, if you are sure of your own virtue and you have power, you have a right and a duty to use it, an extraordinarily un-PC (and very neo-conservative) message. *The Incredibles* was an extended critique of the intolerant egalitarianism of PC, which is the enemy of excellence, and a challenge to people to do the best they can without blaming others for their failings.

In Britain, people are rediscovering their country's extraordinary history, and learning that there is far more to be proud than guilty about. These little rain-swept isles off the west coast of the European peninsula have given an utterly disproportionate amount to the world, including parliamentary democracy, industrialisation and football. Finally, the British are shrugging off politically correct guilt, with even the British Empire being popularly reassessed as not such a bad thing.

But these cracks in the PC edifice could soon close up again. What can be done to ensure the retreat of PC is not just a temporary aberration in the first few years of the twenty-first century? Just as PC embedded itself in the very fabric of the nation by creating armies of NGOs, pressure groups, laws and international treaties to make it almost invulnerable, is there anything that can be done to ensure that PC stays at bay?

In Britain, free speech could be protected with an equivalent of the first amendment in the US Constitution. The state should not try to censor or criminalise any speech unless it is a direct incitement to violence and there is a likelihood that violence will occur as a result. Likewise, democracy can be protected by a law that prohibits the party in government from curbing the activities and membership of other legal democratic political parties.

The oligarchy of political correctors can be curbed by the introduction of direct democracy, such as the citizen's initiatives so popular in the US. Within any legislative area, a binding referendum should be called on any proposal if supported by a certain percentage of the population, so long as the proposal doesn't infringe the basic liberties of individuals, and is fiscally neutral (otherwise people always support tax-cutting measures).

Such citizen's initiatives directly return power to the people, protecting them from being steam-rollered by an elite in hock to political correctness, for example on issues such as the right to defend yourself against intruders in the home, or curbing mass immigration. They provoke far greater political participation by citizens, and in the US have tended to support politically incorrect initiatives (such as curbing the rights of illegal immigrants to welfare) which no mainstream party dared touch.

Such citizens' initiatives are likely to prove very popular and create a far more motivated, less passive and less easily patronised citizenry. Once practiced for a few years, it would be very difficult for a future politically correct government to unravel it, for fear of voter retribution.

Just as PC promoted itself by promoting groups that upheld its values—such as left-wing charities—so unPC groups should also be promoted, representing the interest of ordinary citizens. The interests of taxpayers—and the cause of low taxes—should be presented by a taxpayers' alliance (there is a new, small, and very ineffective one in the UK; there is a far more successful model in the US, which offers financial services, etc.). The interests of homeowners should be represented by a Homeowners Association, offering services to its members and campaigning on the issues that affect them, from council tax to law and order.

The emotional roots of PC must also be challenged. PC is founded on western guilt and self-loathing, which can be countered by more objective teaching of history and western values. Foundations can be set up to preserve and promote Western heritage and values.

To some extent, the rise of the eastern powers, China and India, will ensure in coming decades that western guilt will shrivel: finally having equal powers to compare ourselves too, the West will no longer feel inclined to indulge in self-loathing, but will seek to reaffirm its sense of identity.

To gaze into a crystal ball is to get things wrong, but there is a fair chance that, in the long-run of history, political correctness will be seen as an aberration in Western thought. The product of the uniquely unchallenged position of the West and its unrivalled affluence, the comparative decline of the West compared with the East is likely to spell the demise of political correctness. Finally,

Western minds may be free again to reason rather than just emote, to pursue objective truth rather than subjective virtue.

Epilogue

A Guide to Purging the
Political Correctness Within

Nothing and no one is immune from criticism.

Sidney Hook

The politically correct, in their bid to revolutionise society, taught us that the personal is political. Now that political correctness has become the dominant ideology of society, the tables are turned. It is possible to separate liberalism from dogmatism, to give up political correctness and take up factual correctness, but it can take a personal effort.

1. When you say something in public, ask yourself are you saying it because it is politically correct, or because you know it to be factually correct? Are you choosing intellectual laziness over emotional discomfort?

2. Be open to self-criticism, and criticism from others.

3. Don't psychologise those you disagree with: judge what they say at face value, rather than believing there are hidden, dark motives that entitle you to dismiss what they say without thinking about it.

4. Stick to rational, evidence-based arguments, not discussions of emotionally difficult cases.

5. Feel compassion for 'victims', but don't defer to them. If their victimhood is self-inflicted, deferring to them will only entrench their victimhood, rather than help them.

6. Don't do cultural relativism: stick to a level playing field, and judge everyone by the same ethical standards. Just because someone is a 'victim' or a 'minority' doesn't excuse unethical behaviour that you wouldn't accept in an 'oppressor' or a 'majority'.

7. Don't feel guilty for something you are not responsible for: if you weren't responsible for it, you can't be guilty. Visiting the sins of the fathers on the sons is a contravention of the UN Convention on Human Rights.

8. Don't do guilt by association. Judge people by what they are in themselves, not by their tenuous links to others.

9. Don't do zero tolerance. Humanity is not black and white, but many shades of grey. Thinking in absolutes is not thinking at all.

10. Don't indulge in self-loathing. If you think you should be proud of yourself, and your culture, then be so. Coming from a dominant culture doesn't make you bad.

Many of these points were made far more eminently by the American philosopher Sidney Hook in his essay *The Ethics of Controversy*. His ten rules include declarations that nothing and no one is immune from criticism, and that opponents' arguments should be answered before their motives are impugned. But the last rule is the most pertinent, summing up both the motive and the message for this book:

> The cardinal sin, when we are looking for truth of fact or wisdom of policy, is refusal to discuss, or action which blocks discussion.[1]

Postscript

It was inevitable that a book that attacks the establishment ideology would be attacked as soon as it was published. But what surprised me is how much interest it sparked, how much support it got—and the extent to which the attacks proved much of what I had written. Sometimes, as with the tragically violent demonstrations and death threats from around the Muslim world provoked by the publications of the Mohammed cartoons, the reaction proves the original statement.

The tone was set by a debate I had on the Today programme with the *Independent* newspaper columnist Yasmin Alibhai-Brown, which produced more heat than light. Ms Alibhai-Brown thundered what a shoddy piece of work it was, and demanded to know why I didn't write about the conspiracy of silence surrounding the fact that the overwhelming majority of child molesters in Britain are white men. (Note to Yasmin: Perhaps it's something to do with the fact that the overwhelming majority of child molesters are men, and the overwhelming majority of men in Britain are, er, white. It would only be noteworthy if the overwhelming majority of British child abusers weren't white men.) Both before and after the show, my flagellator refused to speak to me other than to snap at me that I was hysterical and poisonous. Today programme staff were stunned, and told me it rather proved my point—and that many listeners had emailed in saying that her intolerance illustrated well what I had been attempting to say.

But the spat sparked such an extraordinary wave of media interest that TV links vehicles and radio cars queued up outside my flat, and half a dozen columnists waded in. It was clearly an issue where almost everyone had an opinion, and usually a strong one—even radio car operators started cheering me on in agreement, declaring, for example, that 'the truth cannot be racist'. It is to the credit of the BBC that they gave such fair coverage to a book that was at many points critical of it (as the *Daily Mail* pointed out in a news story on this pamphlet.)

The most furious reaction came from the *Independent*, which launched a three-pronged attack, with a news story declaring the pamphlet had caused outrage, its main leader denouncing me, and, yes, a column by Ms Alibhai-Brown, who was clearly keen to have another go.

But this reaction illustrated much of what this pamphlet says about the PC style of debate. The news story, simply based on the fact that I had challenged PC nostrums, illustrated the extent that the PC agenda defines what is newsworthy and what is not—although it did inject some humour, declaring that I was in the grip of 'political incorrectness gone mad'.

The *Independent* leader couldn't have followed PC methodology more if it tried, full of *ad hominem* attacks ('reactionary bilge' etc.), guilt by association and disregard for factual truth. For example, it stated:

> This newspaper does not believe in stifling free speech. Mr Browne is perfectly entitled to attempt to identify a link between the rise in HIV in the UK and African immigration just as people are entitled, we believe, to deny the holocaust. But we reserve the right strongly to disagree with them.[1]

A medical doctor rushed to my defence, pointing out that in the real world, if not the *Independent*'s politically correct one, African immigration actually was the major cause of HIV growth in the UK. He attacked the *Independent* for 'science denial':

> Denying the epidemiology will not allow us to use it wisely in planning health care that responds to the needs of those infected. Denial of science will not help the Africans in the UK living with HIV/Aids to access the services they need. Pretending that it is a distortion of fact, and on a par with the disgraceful practice of holocaust denial, is an equally dangerous practice of science denial

and will result in inappropriate allocation of public health resources.[2]

In her column, Ms Alibhai-Brown also couldn't refrain from the trusty *ad hominem* attacks, saying I fabricate things, was 'disingenuous', 'demented', 'paranoid', had 'horns and a tail' etc. (only one of those is made up), without feeling the need actually to counter my arguments because they were so self-evidently false. Everyone in her world would agree with her, so what's the need? When it came to justifying her denunciation, she just quoted me without the whiff of contrary evidence:

> Here, in his own words, are the fearful fantasies of an anti-PC chap gone quite mad, but who is nevertheless taken as a brave prophet by other paranoids: 'In total, nearly 1,000 people have caught Aids from infected immigrants since Labour came to power, ironically finally giving a rationale to the government's safe sex campaign. That's a 1,000 lives blighted, ultimately, by political correctness... The politically correct truth is publicly proclaimed correct by politicians, celebrities, and the BBC, even if it is wrong, while the factually correct truth is publicly condemned even if it is right.'[3]

I tried to think of a more beautifully ironic, self-defeating, response to my pamphlet, but failed. Apart from the fact that she misquotes me, (confusing Aids with HIV), she illustrates the tactics of the PC of just stating an un-PC view of an opponent as signs of his calumny, and not bothering to let the truth get in the way. It is the mark of established ideologies that they don't feel the need to justify themselves, because they know their assumptions are shared by everyone.

In fact, I had probably rather understated my case. Eventually, nearly two weeks later, and after a bit of prodding, the *Independent* published a letter from me:

> Yasmin Alibhai-Brown misquotes me as saying in my pamphlet on political correctness that 'nearly 1,000 people have caught Aids from infected immigrants since Labour came to power'. In fact, I wrote 'HIV', a rather crucial difference to those affected.

She attacks this as a 'fearful fantasy', but the Health Protection Agency's latest figures show that, since 1998, a total of 1,468 people in the UK have caught HIV from heterosexual sex with people who were themselves infected outside of Europe, the vast majority (thought to be over three quarters) of whom are immigrants to the UK. These cases are largely responsible for the fivefold jump in heterosexual HIV infections in the UK, from 88 cases in 1996 to 466 in 2004.[4]

I also pointed out, in a paragraph they didn't publish, that those most affected were the African community already in Britain, who are at the front line of this imported epidemic, and who are the most harmed by the government's refusal to confront it.

Another scion of the PC establishment, Will Hutton, also denounced me, declaring:

The Civitas pamphlet marshals the usual counter-argument; we are living under the liberal jackboot, self-policing our thoughts, denying ourselves free expression and privileging undeserving minorities etc. All this is paranoid nonsense.[5]

But within days of him writing this there emerged a poignant example of the point I was making: the Metropolitan Police launched an investigation into Sir Iqbal Sacranie, the head of the Muslim Council of Britain, for stating the orthodox Muslim position on homosexuals on a BBC radio programme (he doesn't like them). In a way it was only fair: a couple of weeks earlier, the police had launched an investigation into a Christian family values campaigner, who stated similar views on another BBC radio programme.

What was so ironic about the police investigation of Sir Iqbal is that he was one of the leading forces behind the government's campaign to criminalise incitement to hatred of religion (i.e. in practice, denouncing Islam), punishable by up to seven years in prison.

Here you have the PC dilemma: the government wanting police to investigate attacks on Islam, while they also investigate Muslims for stating orthodox Islamic positions on national radio. This policing of views expressed in broadcasts is an absurdity, an abomination in a country that pretends to believe in free speech, not 'paranoid nonsense'. As a liberal on matters of sexuality, I disagree with Sir Iqbal, but I also defend absolutely his right to say it without being investigated by the bill. The acerbic historian David Starkey pointed up the paradox of the situation in a letter to *The Times*:

> Sir, Twenty-seven Muslim leaders write to you to demand the right, as Muslims, to criticise and denounce homosexuality (letter, Jan 14). As a believer in free speech, I agree. But do they equally agree to my right, as a homosexual and atheist, to criticise and denounce Islam?
>
> And if not, why not?[6]

In the *Evening Standard*, my former colleague Nick Cohen steered clear of all the PC pitfalls, and gave the most civilised critique of this pamphlet declaring 'we are all PC now', and better for it. But his critique was really an agreement—he said, as I did, that PC has helped curb the worst bigotry and discrimination. He also expressed his astonishment at how the BBC fails to cover some inconvenient views, such as African intellectuals denouncing the West for trying to help Africa by further lining the pockets of corrupt African leaders (i.e. giving them more development aid).

Indeed, overall, this pamphlet met with widespread approval, showing that although PC may be the new establishment ideology, there are plenty of subversives willing to question it. On the day that Yasmin Alibhai-Brown dedicated her column to denouncing me, Melanie Philips declared in her column in the *Daily Mail* that this is 'one of the most important pamphlets of recent times', saying that:

> Anthony Browne clearly understands that 'political correctness' is not, as it is so often depicted, some ludicrous absurdity that can be laughed away.[7]

Will Hutton's successor as editor of the *Observer*, the irrepressible Roger Alton, told the *Independent on Sunday* that:

> Anthony Browne is right to point out that some areas in our society are easier to discuss than others, and this is a pity and should be changed.[8]

Peter Horrocks, head of BBC TV news, with clear reference to his own organisation, showed surprising candour:

> There are problems with reporting what are considered to be aberrant views. Consensus can work to exclude certain ideas. It is not about being restricted by external forces, but I think that perhaps people can exclude certain ideas from debate because they do not feel comfortable including them and that they do sometimes limit themselves.[9]

Many others came out in support. Rod Liddle in the *Spectator* said that this pamphlet is 'a polemic against the manner in which intelligent, honest debate is suffocated by political correctness'. Citing some of the examples I mention, he says that 'his analysis, that these are examples of a quite magnificent, deliberately delusional state of mind, seems to me wholly accurate'.

In the *Financial Times*, the veteran commentator, and ever reasonable Martin Wolf, wrote about the government's plan to criminalise incitement to religious hatred:

> the use of the law to protect people from being offended is sure to lead to such absurdities. Moreover, as Anthony Browne, the British journalist, argues in a recent pamphlet, however noble the aims of what its opponents call 'political correctness', it can also too easily lead to the suppression of inconvenient truths. Let a thousand offences bloom, instead, and let people judge freely amongst them.[10]

But the most pleasing accolade came from the iconoclastic philosopher A.C. Grayling, who reviewed this pamphlet in the left-wing *New Statesman*, declaring that it 'mostly persuades'. He said that the principle behind PC is benevolent, in encouraging us to see the best in those who are different from us, but that:

> The pity is that this aim should have become an unacceptable form of policing that has poisoned public debate and made us fools, lest the uncomfortable facts that muddy the clear waters of this principle make anyone think that we do not hold it dear.[11]

I couldn't put it better myself.

Commentary

Commentary

Evidence Supporting Anthony Browne's Table of Truths Suppressed By Political Correctness

David Conway

1. The recent sharp increase in HIV among heterosexuals in the UK has been primarily caused by African immigration, rather than unprotected sex between indigenous teenagers.

In a *Eurosurvelliance* report published at the end of January 2006, G. Elam of the Health Protection Agency Centre for Infections stated that: 'Over 90 per cent of heterosexually acquired HIV infections diagnosed in the UK during 2004 were probably acquired in high prevalence countries of origin, mainly sub-Saharan Africa.' Elam went on to note that:

> The annual number of infections newly diagnosed in heterosexual men and women born in sub-Saharan Africa remains high at 3,136 in 2004. There has also been a slow but steady rise in the number of heterosexual infections probably acquired in the UK in recent years, from 227 in 2000 to 498 in 2004. Most of these individuals were probably infected by partners who were themselves presumed to have been infected outside Europe, mainly in Africa. As the number of black and minority ethnic heterosexuals living with HIV (diagnosed and undiagnosed) in the UK grows, the likelihood of heterosexual transmission within the UK will increase.[1]

2. The cause of the pay-gap in the UK is not the result of women suffering sex-discrimination in the workplace but of their own lifestyle choices.

The average earnings of women in the UK are 20 per cent less than those of men. Catherine Hakim, labour economist at the London School of Economics, has developed

101

the so-called 'preference theory' to support her contention that this pay-gap is less the result of women suffering from sex discrimination in the work-place than of their own lifestyle preferences.

According to this theory, the pay-gap between the two sexes is not caused by women suffering sex discrimination in the work-place, since this has been eradicated from the work-place since the 1970s when anti-discrimination legislation, equal pay and comparable worth were all introduced. Rather, what accounts for the pay-gap, according to Hakim's theory, is the fact that, upon their becoming parents, many women have chosen to subordinate their careers, either wholly or partially, to their parental and domestic roles and responsibilities. The result is that many more women than men have chosen temporarily to withdraw from the labour market or to confine themselves to part-time work for the sake of raising and looking after their children.

Evidence that the different priorities of men and women towards work and domestic responsibilities—which is the immediate cause of the pay-gap between them—results from their genuinely different choices, rather than women-unfriendly labour-market practices, is supplied by Sweden. There a similar pay-gap exists between men and women, despite Swedish law obliging employers to offer their male and female employees equal and generous paid paternity and maternity leave upon becoming parents. It was found that Swedish men did not want to take up these parental leave opportunities nearly as much did Swedish women. According to Patricia Morgan:

> In 1995, one month of Swedish parental leave was earmarked for the father, since mothers were using most days (90 per cent or more in 1993-96). Despite all the propaganda and various pressures, men do not usually take parental leave... Most mothers prefer not to share the care of a newborn with the father. So men [we]re made to 'care', like it or not... The new rule made little impact. By the late 1990s, fathers were still taking only 11 per cent of leave days, and half took none at all. Most of those men who

took it worked in the public sector and had wives in high-status jobs. Despite all the enthusiasm for Swedish role reversal in the UK press, it is not even a reality in Sweden, only rhetoric.[2]

Of the pay-gap more generally, Hakim has observed: 'It's nothing to do with sex discrimination, but the recognition that you cannot have two major life projects—work and family—and give them both as much attention as they deserve'.[3] Certainly, the attitudinal surveys she has undertaken of European men and women have revealed that many more women than men value spending time at home looking after their children in comparison with pursuing a paid career. Hakim found that: '[o]verall a two-thirds majority of European men and women favour the idea of the working wife and a two-thirds majority favour the wife retaining all or the major part of the domestic role'.[4]

The pay differential between the sexes can be fully accounted for by reference to the differences between them in their respective preferences in relation to paid work and familial and domestic responsibilities. As Hakim once stated:

The bottom line is that, as far as investment in a career is concerned … [t]he major investment required is one of time and effort. [I]f you are seriously interested in a career, you don't have time for children and if you are seriously interested in bringing up more than one child, let's say, you don't have the time, effort and imagination for getting to the top of a career. The fact is that children are a 20-year project and a career a 20- to 40-year project and there is an incompatibility there… You can have one child and be a nominal mother […so as to] concentrate on your career. But once you have two children or more what you are far more likely to want is work that is interesting and challenging and that fits in with the children—that allows you to work certain hours and not be bothered at all times of the day and night by a very demanding employer.[5]

In sum, women are more child-oriented than are men and that difference is enough to account for the pay-gap between them.

3. The policy of multiculturalism in the UK has indirectly contributed to the manufacture there of its home-grown suicide bombers.

Few assertions are more difficult to verify empirically than are those positing a causal connection between some particular social phenomenon, or set of such phenomena, such as the London suicide bombings on the one hand, and, on the other, some other social phenomenon or set of social phenomena, such as the adoption in recent years of multiculturalism as a favoured government policy. Thus, there is little by way of empirical data to prove that, had the policy of multiculturalism not been pursued with as much enthusiasm as it has been in the UK by central and local government these last 30 or so years, the London suicide bombings would never have happened.

Notwithstanding, the claim that multiculturalism contributed towards bringing about the atrocities is one that has been made by several commentators with an 'insider's knowledge' of the minority communities from which the London bombers came. The essential way in which the policy has been implicated in the bombings is by being claimed to have helped create social conditions favourable towards the cultivation of a generation of British-born Muslim men deeply alienated from their non-Muslim compatriots. The segregated upbringing towards which multiculturalism contributed left many of them so disconnected from mainstream British society as to be susceptible to radicalisation by Islamists to the point at which they were ready and willing to 'martyr' themselves for their religion in acts of suicide-bombing.

Some had warned that multiculturalism was creating social conditions especially favourable to the radicalisation of Muslim youth, with dire consequences in store, for several years before the 7 July bombings. In the wake of riots of Muslim youths in the summer of 2001 in the towns of Oldham, Burnley, and Bradford, the Home Office commissioned a report on their underlying causes from a panel under the chairmanship of Ted Cantle. The so-called Cantle report, published in December of that year, concluded that the riots occurred because the rioters had been alienated from and made hostile towards their non-Muslim compatriots by having been physically and culturally segregated from them as a result of the adoption of multiculturalism as an official policy for the previous 20 years.

The policy of multiculturalism had first been adopted in response to an earlier wave of riots by ethnic minorities in Britain that had occurred at the beginning of and during the 1970s. As Kenan Malik observed in an article entitled 'The trouble with multiculturalism', published in December 2001, following and in response to these riots:

> Local authorities in inner-city areas... pioneered a new strategy of making [minority] communities feel part of British society... At the heart of the strategy was a redefinition of racism. Racism now meant not simply the denial of equal rights but the denial of the right to be different. Black people, many argued, should not be forced to accept British values, or to adopt a British identity. Rather, different peoples should have the right to accept their identities, explore their own histories, formulate their own values, pursue their own lifestyles.[6]

A case in point, for Malik, was the way the Bradford municipal authorities had responded to the rioting by Asian youths there in the 1970s by shortly thereafter embracing the policy of multiculturalism. As he explained:

> A 12-point race relations plan declared Bradford to be a 'multiracial, multicultural city', and stated that every section of the community had 'an equal right to maintain its own identity, culture, language, religion and customs'.[7]

By the mid-1980s, the effect upon Bradford of its having implemented this policy of multiculturalism was to have brought about the segregation of the city along religious lines. Its various different Asian communities,

Hindu, Sikh and Muslim, had become increasingly separated from and at odds with each other as well as with their host community. All groups had now begun to compete against each other for public funding, with the authorities tending to favour the more conservative leaders of these religious groups who tended to accentuate their group's own particularities, and thereby further to encourage segregation.

In his 2001 article, Malik only went so far as to suggest that multiculturalism had resulted in 'not a greater sensitivity to cultural difference but an indifference to other people's lives'. By 2004, others had begun to suggest that the policy had been far more subversive of inter-communal harmony. In April of that year, Munira Mirza claimed that, by having evacuated from the idea of Britishness any value-content other than the meta-value of tolerance, 'the creed of multiculturalism has turned away a generation of British Muslims and made them sympathetic to the cause of religious fundamentalism'.[8]

It was a severe and extreme form of alienation that led four young British-born Muslim men one morning in July 2005 to blow themselves up simultaneously on three different London underground trains and on a bus, taking with their own lives those of 53 of their fellow passengers. Whatever might have been the precise motive of the bombers, the segregation of their co-religionists from mainstream British society that multiculturalism had helped to create was soon claimed to be among the factors responsible for the alienation that had made it possible for them to be radicalised to the point of undertaking the bombings.

In an article published in *The Times* on 16 July 2005, entitled 'Multiculturalism has fanned the flames of Islamic extremism', Kenan Malik claimed that multiculturalism had 'helped to create a tribal Britain with no political or moral centre' which had offered a generation of young

British-born Muslims nothing to identify with beyond their religion. He added:

> The politics of ideology has given way to the politics of identity, creating a more fragmented Britain… where many groups assert their identity through a sense of victimhood and grievance. This has been especially true of Muslim communities… [M]any Muslim leaders have nurtured an exaggerated sense of victimhood for their own political purposes. The result has been to stoke up anger and resentment, creating a siege mentality that… has helped to transform a small number of young men into savage terrorists.[9]

Munira Mirza has also expressed her opinion that the London bombings had been made more likely as a result of multiculturalism:

> I think 7/7 awakened a lot of people to one of the big problems with multiculturalism, which is that it doesn't actually defend anything. I think the terrorists were looking for meaning too. They can't find it here; being British is so discredited in this country that they look for that identity elsewhere. But the most compelling thing about the al-Qaeda identity is its victimhood status; it is the ultimate logic of multiculturalism, with its claim that it represents an oppressed minority.[10]

4. The recent increase in anti-Semitic incidents reported throughout Europe has been largely due to attacks upon Jews carried out by Muslim youths rather than white neo-Nazis.

Since 2000, there has been a marked increase throughout Europe in the number of attacks upon Jews on account of their religion or ethnicity. The main perpetrators of these attacks appear to have been Muslim youths rather than white neo-Nazis, who are more given to attacking the property of Jews, such as their synagogues and cemeteries, rather than their persons. This has been the finding of both the US Department of State and of the British-based Stephen Roth Institute for the Study of Anti-Semitism and Racism.

At the beginning of 2005, the US State Department submitted to the US Congressional Committee on Foreign

Relations and the Committee on International Relations a report on Global Anti-Semitism for the 18-month period between July 2003 and the end of December 2004. The report began by noting 'the increasing frequency and severity of anti-Semitic incidents since the start of the twenty-first century, particularly in Europe'.[11] The report then continued:

> The disturbing rise of anti-Semitic intimidation and incidents is widespread throughout Europe... The Vienna-based European Union Monitoring Centre (EUMC), for 2002 and 2003, identified France, Germany, the United Kingdom, Belgium, and the Netherlands as EU member countries with notable increases in incidents...
>
> In Western Europe, traditional far-right groups still account for a significant proportion of the attacks against Jews and Jewish properties; disadvantaged and disaffected Muslim youths increasingly were responsible for most of the other incidents.[12]

The report linked the increase in the number of anti-Semitic incidents in European countries to the intensifying conflicts in the Middle East. In Belgium, it stated, 'the annual number of complaints rose to 30 between 2000 and 2003; prior to 1999, an average of four anti-Semitic incidents were registered per year. There were 40 complaints filed in the first 11 months of the year [2004]'.[13]

In France, 510 anti-Semitic incidents were reported to have occurred in the first six months of 2004, as compared with 593 for all of 2003. The French National Consultative Commission on Human Rights was reported to have claimed that 'disaffected French North-African youths were responsible for many of the incidents... A small number of incidents were also attributed to extreme-right and extreme-left organisations.'[14]

In Germany, it reported that, while in 2003 'the total number of registered anti-Semitic crimes decreased to 1,199 (from 1,515 in 2002)... the number of violent crimes increased from 28 to 35, and the number of desecrations of Jewish cemeteries, synagogues or memorials went up from 78 to 115... Leading politicians from all major parties continued to assert that neo-Nazi groups posed a serious threat to public order. On the other hand, some observers blamed the actions in the Middle East for rising anti-Semitism.'[15]

The statistics that the US State Department report provided about the United Kingdom did not allow for any inter-temporal comparisons. The report merely noted that, between July 2003 and June 2004, 511 anti-Semitic incidents had been recorded by the Community Security Trust, an organisation in the UK that analyses threats to the Jewish community there and co-ordinates with British police to provide Jewish institutions with protection.[16]

However, in its annual report on anti-Semitism for the year 2004, the Stephen Roth Institute does provides statistical data about anti-Semitic incidents in the UK in that year, from which some reliable inferences may be drawn as to the likely identity of their perpetrators. The report describes 2004 as having been 'the worst in terms of the number, frequency and nature of anti-Semitic expressions and events since the outbreak of the current wave of anti-Semitism in October 2000'.[17] After noting a very marked increase in 2004 in the number of 'attacks on individual Jews by persons acting spontaneously', the report went on to claim these attacks had been 'perpetrated typically by young politically unaffiliated immigrants, mostly but not only from Muslim countries; vandalism of Jewish property and communal institutions [being] ... generally carried out by extreme rightists'.[18]

The report goes on to observe that:

In the UK, the number of major violent incidents rose from 50 in 2003 to 84 in 2004. The CST (Community Security Trust) tallied a total of 532 anti-Semitic events, the highest number since 1984, marking an increase of 42 per cent from 2003 to 2004 (compared with 15 per cent from 2002 to 2003). Physical aggression was a leading category, replacing to a certain extent that of arson attacks against synagogues which marked the years 2001-2003.[19]

As to the identity of the perpetrators of the anti-Semitic incidents across Europe more generally in 2004, the Stephen Roth Institute report offered three reasons for supposing Muslim youths more likely to have been responsible for their increased number than white neo-Nazis. First, it reported, when assailants had been identified at all by their victims, they had tended to be 'described as "young Muslims", "young Asians", or "young North Africans"... It is unlikely [victims] would confuse them with "young white males"'.[20] Second, the percentage of physical assaults against Jewish individuals had increased dramatically by comparison with Jewish cemetery and synagogue desecrations. The report noted that, while 'the number of cases in which the police succeeded in establishing an identification of the perpetrators of physical attacks is significantly small, the involvement of Arabs, Muslims or members of other ethnic minorities in those acts was much higher than that of members of the extreme right'.[21] Third, adding further weight to the suggestion that Muslims had been principally behind the increased number of attacks on Jews in Europe, the report observed that 'over the last few years, and even in the 1990s, there has been clear indication of a link between tensions in the Middle East and the rise in anti-Semitic manifestations in western Europe'.[22]

That Muslims, rather than neo-Nazis, have been primarily responsible for the recent increase in anti-Semitic incidents in Europe is also the opinion of Robert Wistrich, Professor of Modern European and Jewish History at the Hebrew University of Jerusalem and director of its International Centre for the Study of anti-Semitism. In an interview published by the Jerusalem Centre for Public Affairs in October 2004, Professor Wistrich remarked:

All researchers know that, in several West European countries, young radicalised Muslims are the major perpetrators of anti-Semitic acts. This is the case not only in France, but also in Belgium, the Netherlands, Sweden, and increasingly in Great Britain ... Since far-right radicalism in Germany is still quite a significant factor, the balance of anti-Semitism [there] is different.[23]

5. The educational underachievement of black school-boys in the UK is due more to their glorification of a deviant lifestyle than their having been subjected to racial discrimination.

Writing about the comparative educational performance of Britain's various different ethnic minorities, BBC Education Correspondent Mike Baker observed in 2002:

> Probably the greatest concern is over pupils, especially boys, of African and Caribbean origin. This concern extends beyond examination performance to issues of discipline and motivation.

> The proportion of African-Caribbean students achieving five good GCSE grades is well below the national average ... [Moreover] pupils of African-Caribbean origin are several times more likely to be expelled than whites of the same gender.[24]

The cause of the relatively poor performance of Afro-Caribbean pupils, especially boys, has been much debated. Some have suggested that their poor performance is the result of their having suffered adverse discrimination on account of their colour. However, since children of Indian and Chinese extraction have been found consistently to out-perform their white counterparts in British schools, and since Afro-Caribbean girls have also consistently outperformed white boys in these schools, this suggestion strains credibility.

Two prominent blacks on the left of the political spectrum in British politics have both proffered an alternative explanation for the comparatively poor performance of black British schoolboys. It is one that attaches far more importance as a causal factor of their poor educational performance to their own propensity to glorify a life of deviancy.

In a special report on the subject published in the *Observer* on 20 August 2000, Trevor Phillips, chair of the Commission for Racial Equality, observed that, having successfully thrown off the shackles of slavery, the Afro-Caribbean community in Britain was in danger of entering the twenty-first century 'tempted to volunteer for a new kind of bondage—a subtle psychological entrapment that the late Bob Marley called "mental slavery"'. Phillips went on:

> Coming from 'the street' is the latest test of authenticity for us. We are only genuinely black if we speak Jamaican, wear expensive designer clothes and reject anything that resembles formal education or scholarship... For many young black men it is easier to take the route of 'gold chains, no brains' than to battle the bias of school, street and workplace.[25]

Phillips reiterated this opinion in a BBC television programme on the subject that was broadcast in March 2005. In it, he called for black boys to be taught in schools separately from white boys in order to 'reduce the cultural and peer pressure that told them that being clever was unfashionable'.[26]

That it was their own voluntary embrace of a culture of deviancy, rather than their having been subjected to racial discrimination at school, that accounted for the poor educational performance of black British males was also a view espoused by Lee Jasper, chair of the National Assembly Against Racism and an adviser to the mayor of London. In an article published in the *Observer* in February 2002, Jasper painted the following bleak picture of their plight:

> Around 45 per cent of London's unemployed are black. Failure rates among black schoolchildren are the silent catastrophe of London. The black prison population in Britain has doubled since 1994... Young black men occupy more than 40 per cent of the psychiatry beds in London. Teenage pregnancy rates are the

highest in Europe and the number of single parents is going through the roof... Sexually transmitted diseases, especially HIV, also have a disproportionate impact on the black community. [27]

Jasper was no less forthright in his assessment of the cause of these problems:

> Young black men have found alternative validation and support among peers whose creed is 'live rich, live fast and don't give a damn about society'. At its most basic this is manifested in a street 'gangsta'; or 'ghetto fabulous' iconography played out in school playgrounds. But at its most extreme it is about an underground criminal economy founded in guns and drugs and now spilling over into the mainstream. [28]

6. Poverty in Africa has been caused by misrule rather than insufficient aid.

There is one startling fact that is beyond all contention concerning international aid to Africa. This fact is that, despite its having received, comparatively speaking, enormous quantities of aid over the past half-century, poverty on that continent has not diminished but rather increased. Thus, as has been noted recently: 'In the past 30 years aid as a percentage of Africa's gross domestic product has more than trebled, while in the same period economic growth has collapsed from two per cent to zero.' [29]

The quantity of aid that Africa has received over this period should, in theory, have been enough to have enabled serious progress to be made in reducing the scale of poverty there, but this has conspicuously failed to happen. In the absence of any attested alternative, one plausible explanation of why the scale of poverty has not diminished in Africa in this time, despite all the aid it has received, is that much of it has been diverted by those ruling many of the countries from the intended recipients to themselves. Certainly, the scale of corruption and misrule in many African countries since they were granted independence has been notably great and more than sufficient to account for the continuing poverty of so many parts of that continent.

Recent presidents of Nigeria, Zambia and Malawi have tried to stamp out corruption in their countries, but have had great difficulty in doing so. As Jeremy Pope, a founding executive director of the anticorruption watchdog Transparency International has said: 'What has been revealed is a hopelessly corrupt political elite—a political class across the spectrum that sees politics as a way of becoming wealthy.'[30]

That it has been corruption and domestic misrule in Africa, rather than insufficient aid that has been the prime reason for poverty remaining so endemic and widespread is borne out by the relative economic and political success that Botswana has enjoyed. As Jeremy Pope observed of that country's ruling elite: 'They look after their money, they invest wisely, and they run a decent country with a very good human rights record.'[31]

That attempts to reduce poverty in Africa have failed because of misrule and corruption is a view publicly espoused by two African economists: James Shikwati of Kenya and Thompson Ayodele, director of the Institute of Public Policy Analysis based in Lagos, Nigeria.

In an interview that he gave to *Der Spiegel* in July 2005, Shikwato made a plea for the west to stop giving aid to Africa, as it only made matters worse in his view:

> The countries that have collected the most development aid are also the ones that are in the worst shape. Despite the billions that have been poured into Africa, the continent remains poor. [This is because] huge bureaucracies are financed (with the aid money), corruption and complacency are promoted, [and] Africans are taught to be beggars and not to be independent. In addition, development aid weakens the local markets everywhere and dampens the spirit of entrepreneurship that we so desperately need. As absurd as it may sound: development aid is one of the reasons for Africa's problems.[32]

Shikwato's opinions were echoed by Ayodele. On the day of the Gleneagles summit last July, when debts of African countries were written-off, Ayodele issued a press release through his Institute on the subject of aid to Africa. In it he asserted that:

> Africa's lack of development... does not stem from lack of funds. More foreign aid will not eliminate poverty and launch African countries to productivity and growth... [A]id does not trickle down to the miserable people that we see daily on our televisions and who really need it; instead, it provides incentives for mis-governance, propping up dictators, encouraging corruption, fin-ancing projects that are irrelevant to ordinary people and making investments which cost billions of dollars in aid money... Far from fixing Africa's problems, aid worsens it. Growth does not depend in the amount of aid a country gets but on factors which can only be built up by governments in Africa. These factors include adequate protection for property rights, effective institutions, clear and enforceable rules which are predictable, an efficient and prompt judicial system and, above all, freedom to trade.[33]

Notes

1: What is Political Correctness?

1   Coleman, P., 'What is Political Correctness? The Pros and Cons', *Quadrant Magazine*, Australia, March 2000.

2   Coleman, 'What is Political Correctness? The Pros and Cons', 2000.

3   Weyrich, P., open letter from Free Congress Foundation, 16 February 1999. Letter reported in the *Washington Post*, 18 February 1999, in article headlined: 'Key Conservative Surrenders in Culture War'.

4   Lind, W.S., 'The Origins of Political Correctness', address to 13th Accuracy in Academia conference, George Washington University, 10 July 1998.

5   Lind, 'The Origins of Political Correctness', 1998.

6   Bernstein, R., 'The rising hegemony of the politically correct', *New York Times*, 29 October 1990.

7   Safire, W., *Safire's New Political Dictionary*, Random House, 1993.

8   Editorial, *Wall Street Journal*, 31 December 1993.

9   Ibsen, H., *The Master Builder*, Act 3, 1892.

10 *Independent*, 1 April 2004.

11 *Daily Telegraph*, 1 April 2004.

2: The Hallmarks of Political Correctness

1   Sowell, T., *A Conflict of Visions*, Basic Books, 2002, p. 10.

2   Forsyth, F., 'Why political correctness is the enemy of the people', *Daily Express*, 6 February 2004.

3   Aitkenhead, D., 'Their homophobia is our fault: real liberals would realise it is meaningless to vilify Jamaicans for attitudes that Britain created', *Guardian,* 5 January 2005.

4   Berkeley, R., 'We won't desert them: Jamaica must take responsibility for its homophobia', *Guardian*, 11 January 2005.

5   Tatchell, P., 'An embrace that shames London', *New Statesman*, 24 January 2005.

3: The Origins of Political Correctness

1   Lind, W.S., *Political Correctness: A Short History of an Ideology*, Free Congress Foundation, November 2004.

2   Coleman, P., 'What is Political Correctness? The Pros and Cons', *Quadrant Magazine*, Australia, March 2000.

3   Forsyth, F., 'Why political correctness is the enemy of the people', *Daily Express*, 6 February 2004.

4   Ellis, J., *Literature Lost: Social Agendas and the Corruption of Humanities*, Yale University Press, 1997,   p. 15.

5   Schwartz, H., 'The Psychodynamics of Political Correctness', *Journal of Applied Behavioral Science*, 33 (2), 1997.

4: The Triumph of Political Correctness

1   Weyrich, P., Letter to Conservatives, Free Congress Foundation, 1999.

2   D'Souza, D., Illiberal Education: The Politics of Race and Sex on Campus, The Free Press, 1991, p. 2.

3   Coleman, P., 'What is Political Correctness? The Pros and Cons', *Quadrant Magazine*, Australia, March 2000.

4   Lind, W.S., *Political Correctness: A Short History of an Ideology*, Free Congress Foundation, 2004, p. 5.

5   Shapiro, H., University of Cincinnati, presentation to 18th International Congress of Historical Sciences, Montreal, August 1995.

6   Ellis, J., *Literature Lost: Social Agendas and the Corruption of Humanities*, Yale University Press, 1997.

5: The Benefits of Political Correctness

1   Roxburgh, A., *Preachers of Hate*, Gibson Square Books, 2002, p. 302.

6: The Drawbacks of Political Correctness

1 Alhibai-Brown, Y., *Evening Standard,* 24 June 2002.

2 Browne, A., '"Myth" of Chernobyl suffering exposed', *Observer,* 6 January 2002.

3 Schwartz, H., 'The Psychodynamics of Political Correctness', *Journal of Applied Behavioral Science,* 33 (2), 1997.

4 Rushdie, S., 'Democracy is no polite tea party', *Los Angeles Times,* 7 February 2005.

5 Mill, J. S., *On Liberty* (1859), Oxford University Press, 1991, p. 20.

6 BBC Radio 4 Today Programme, website report, 1 January 2004.

7 Bennett, J.C., United Press International Column, 5 April 2002.

7: How Political Correctness Affects Policies

1 Wilson, J.Q., interview with *American Enterprise Online,* June 2001.

9: The Dissidents from Political Correctness

1 Horowitz, D., 'The Era of Progressive Witch-Hunts', in *Left Illusions: An Intellectual Odyssey,* Spence Publishing, October 2003, p. 230.

2 Horowitz, D., 'The Road to Nowhere', in *Left Illusions: An Intellectual Odyssey,* 1990, p. 126.

3 Horowitz, D., 'Nicaragua: A Speech to My Former Comrades on the Left', in *Commentary Magazine,* June 1986, p. 27.

Epilogue

1 Hook, S., 'The Ethics of Controversy', included in *Philosophy and Public Policy,* Southern Illinois University Press, 1980.

Postscript

1 *Independent,* leader, 4 January 2006.

2   Harding, Dr R., Lecturer, Department of Palliative Care and
    Policy, King's College London School of Medicine, *Independent*,
    6 January 2006.

3   Alibhai-Brown, Y., *Independent*, 9 January 2006.

4   Browne, A., *Independent*, 21 January 2006.

5   Hutton, W., *Observer*, 8 January 2006.

6   Starkey, D., *The Times*, 16 January 2006.

7   Phillips, M., *Daily Mail*, 9 January 2006.

8   Alton, R., *Independent on Sunday*, 8 January 2006.

9   Horrocks, P., *Independent on Sunday*, 8 January 2006.

10 Wolf, M., *Financial Times*, 8 February 2006.

11 Grayling, A.C., *New Statesman*, 23 January 2006.

Commentary

1   Elam, G., 'HIV and AIDS in the United Kingdom African
    communities: guidelines produced for prevention and care',
    Eurosurveillance Weekly Release, Vol. 11, Issue 1, 28 January
    2006. http://www.eurosurveillance.org/ew/2006/060126.asp#5

2   Morgan, P., *Family Policy, Family Changes: Sweden, Italy and
    Britain Compared*, London: Civitas, 2006, p. 33.

3   McFadden, J., 'The perils of having it all', *The Scotsman*, 2
    February 2005.
    http://living.scotsman.com/index.cfm?id=122492005

4   Hakim, C., 'The Sexual Division of Labour and Women's
    Heterogeneity', *British Journal of Sociology*, Vol. 47, No. 1,
    March 1996, 178-88, 181.

5   Quoted in Moorhead, J., 'For decades we've been told Sweden is a
    great place to be a working parent. But we've been duped',
    Guardian, 22 September 2004.
    http://www.guardian.co.uk/g2/story/0,,1309724,00.html

6   Malik, K., 'The trouble with multiculturalism', *Spiked Online*,
    18 December 2001, p. 3.
    http://www.spiked-online.com/Articles/00000002D35E.htm

7   Malik, 'The trouble with multiculturalism', 2001, p. 3.

THE RETREAT OF REASON

8   Mirza, M., 'Backlash against multiculturalism' *Spiked Online*,
    7 April 2004.
    http://www.spiked-online.com/Articles/0000000CA4C4.htm

9   Malik, K., 'Multiculturalism has fanned the flames of Islamic
    extremism', *The Times*, 16 July 2005.
    http://www.timesonline.co.uk/article/0,,1072-1695604,00.html

10 Quoted in Therisa, A., 'Multi what?' *Total: Spec Magazine*, April
    2006, p. 92.

11 *Report on Global Anti-Semitism between 1 July 2003 and 15
    December 2004*, submitted by the US Department of State to the
    Committee on Foreign Relations and the Committee on
    International Relations, released by the Bureau of Democracy,
    Human Rights, and Labour, 5 January 2005, p. 1.
    http://www.state.gov/g/drl/rls/40258.htm

12 *Report on Global Anti-Semitism between 1 July 2003 and 15
    December 2004*, 2005, p. 2.

13 *Report on Global Anti-Semitism between 1 July 2003 and 15
    December 2004*, 2005, p. 9.

14 *Report on Global Anti-Semitism between 1 July 2003 and 15
    December 2004*, 2005, p. 13.

15 *Report on Global Anti-Semitism between 1 July 2003 and 15
    December 2004*, 2005, pp. 15-16.

16 *Report on Global Anti-Semitism between 1 July 2003 and 15
    December 2004*, 2005, p. 35.

17 Stephen Roth Institute for the Study of Antisemitism and Racism,
    Annual Report for 2004, p. 1.
    http://www.tau.ac.il/Anti-Semitism/asw2004/general-analysis.htm

18 Stephen Roth Institute for the Study of Antisemitism and Racism,
    Annual Report for 2004.

19 Stephen Roth Institute for the Study of Antisemitism and Racism,
    Annual Report for 2004, p. 2.

20 Stephen Roth Institute for the Study of Antisemitism and Racism,
    Annual Report for 2004, p. 8.

21 Stephen Roth Institute for the Study of Antisemitism and Racism,
    Annual Report for 2004, pp. 8-9.

22 Stephen Roth Institute for the Study of Antisemitism and Racism, Annual Report for 2004.

23 'Something is Rotten in the State of Europe: Anti-Semitism as a Civilizational Pathology: An interview with Robert Wistrich', *Jerusalem Centre for Public Affairs*, No. 25, 1 October 2004, 1-10, p. 7. http://goldwater.mideastreality.com/2004/sep/27_06.html

24 Baker, M., 'Educational achievement', *BBC News*, Race UK 2002. http://news.bbc.co.uk/hi/english/static/in_depth/uk/2002/race/educ ational_achi...

25 Phillips, T., 'The myth of gold chains and no brains', *Observer*, 20 August 2000. http://www.guardian.co.uk/racism/Story/0,2763,356554,00.html

26 'Segregation in UK Schools', *Raising Kids*, 7 March 2005. http://www.raisingkids.co.uk/todaysnews_070305_01.asp

27 Jasper, L., 'Breaking out of the black "gangsta" ghetto', *Observer* 17 February 2002. http://observer.guardian.co.uk/race/story/0,11255,651769,00.html

28 Jasper, 'Breaking out of the black "gangsta" ghetto', 2002.

29 Ruddock, A., 'Waving chequebooks won't do anything to end poverty', *Sunday Times*, 19 June 2005. http://www.timesonline.co.uk/article/0,,2091-1660070,00.html

30 Gidley-Kitchen, V., 'Is corruption getting worse in Africa?', BBC News, 2 November 2005. http://news.bbc.co.uk/go/em/fr/-/2/hi/africa/4254845.stm

31 Gidley-Kitchen, 'Is corruption getting worse in Africa?', 2005.

32 'For God's Sake, Please Stop the Aid!', *Der Spiegel*, 4 July 2005. http://www.sopiegel.de/international/spielgel/0,151`8,363663,00. html

33 Ayodele, T., 'Doubling of Foreign Aid to Africa will not lead to a Take-off into Self-sustained Growth' Press Release, *Institute of Public Policy Analysis*, Nigeria, 6 July 2005.

http://ippanigeria.org/page.php?instructions=page&page_id=534& nav_id=87